CRITICISM IN YOUR LIFE

CRITICISM IN YOUR LIFE

How to Give It—
How to Take It—
How to Make It Work for You

Dr. Deborah Bright

MASTER
MEDIA
LIMITED
New York

MASTERMEDIA and colophon are registered trademarks of
MasterMedia Limited

Library of Congress Cataloging-in-Publication Data

Bright, Deborah.
    Criticism in your life.

    1. Criticism, Personal.   I. Title.
BF637.C74B75   1988   158'.1   88-23125
ISBN 0-942361-20-2

Designed by Irving Perkins Associates
Manufactured in the United States of America

10   9   8   7   6   5   4   3   2   1

First paperback printing July 1990

To the one I cherish most,
and always enjoy being with,
my husband, Paul

ACKNOWLEDGMENTS

My sincere thanks to those who gave of their time and shared their experiences to illustrate vividly the points I make throughout the book.

Special thanks are extended to the following people for their valuable contributions: Bernice Malamud, Robert Levit, Ellen Sills Levy, Kim Kostere, Patricia Funcie, Bill Holden, Ken Hines, Dave Gerhards, Arla Goldblum, Peter Cummings, Renee Ross, Mark Landsberg, Joyce Daza, Danielle Jagalla, Myrna Weiss, Glenny Tubbs, Gary Banus, Logan Cockrun, Karen Schloss, John Sturman, Alan Blank, Marvin Tarplin, Judith Briles, Peter Kenning, Frank Stanton, Alan Wheeler, Suzanne Lulewicz, and Jenesta Marlin.

I would like to extend my appreciation to my hairdresser, Richard Biondi, and to my parents, Saul and Doris Tomberg, who, although they do not appear in the book, listened patiently and contributed endless hours of support to this endeavor. And of course, Dr. Tessa Warschaw, who helped to make this all happen.

I am indebted to my publisher, Susan Stautberg, my editor, Elithea Whittaker, and, most importantly, to my husband, Paul, for his ongoing support as my favorite critic.

CONTENTS

AUTHOR'S PREFACE

I first began thinking seriously about criticism and how it affects our lives about twenty years ago. At that time I was ranked among the top ten women divers in the U.S. One day during a practice and shortly before the 1968 Olympic Trials, my coach seemed relentlessly "on my case"—to the point where it didn't seem I could do anything right. It dawned on me while climbing exhausted up the ten meter platform ladder that I really did not resent the harsh barrage of criticism from my coach while if anyone else tried to change my behavior with such vindictiveness I would either be very angry or emotionally destroyed. What was it that made the coach's critical ranting tolerable while others who criticized me often caused resentful reactions?

The answer came quickly—the coach shared my goal and ambition to achieve. The coach was yelling and criticizing me in an effort to change my behavior so I would succeed. I knew that his motivation was honest and genuine and I appreciated his concern with what I was doing wrong as much as I appreciated his praise for what I did right. I discussed my thoughts with many of my colleagues and other athletes and all of them—yes, every single one of them—agreed that criticism from their coach was something that helped them. Therefore they did not resent it.

Is the relationship that an athlete shares with his coach unique? Is it possible that criticism communicated elsewhere from poolside or the playing field can also be accepted and perceived as a mutual effort to achieve rather than a communicated cornerstone of confrontation and long-term resentment? I think it is possible and have wondered why so many bosses, parents, lovers and friends are reluctant to communicate the "negative" honestly. Are they afraid of creating resentment or of irredeemably destroying their relationships?

The years following my career as a diver were dedicated to studying and identifying the factors which affect performance. Much of my research and attention focused on the area of stress and how it affects performance and the achievement of our goals and objectives. The findings led to the writing of what is now the leading selling book on stress: *Creative Relaxation: Turning Your Stress into Positive Energy*. It wasn't too long into my professional career as a speaker, educator and counselor in the area of stress that it became extremely evident that a significant source of stress for many of my clients was rooted in a complex syndrome involving poor communication of expectations and difficulty in handling criticism.

Most of us have a difficult time with criticism, whether giving it or receiving it. Few of us have formulated any method or design for sorting out criticism that we should act on from criticism we should simply ignore. In the absence of any kind of logic to apply to dealing with criticism, whether from others or ourselves, we have few alternatives but to react emotionally to those who criticize us—bosses, subordinates, parents, children, in-laws, neighbors, friends, ourselves and you name it.

Likewise, because we don't understand the characteristics of "quality criticism" or how to differentiate it from malicious abuse, we hesitate over, if not avoid completely, giving criticism to those who can surely benefit from it. By learning how to take criticism and to give it effectively we can achieve our goals more quickly. We can influence others in an acceptable and appreciated way with a minimum amount of stress and emotional catastrophe. Criticism is, in fact, the most powerful communication device for bringing about change in the behavior of others and ourselves. Yet it is a subject most of us rarely think about.

Years ago, when I first began to seriously research the subject of criticism, I was surprised to find that the time needed to scan the subject required little more than an afternoon in the New York Public Library. Outside of a few personal articles on such things as "how to criticize your lover," there was virtually an empty shelf. As a result, I decided to conduct my own survey in coordination with Simmons Market Research Bureau. Together we explored what Americans think about criticism. After surveying and interviewing over 500 managers, professionals, parents, children, athletes, military officers and politicians of all ages and all dispositions—what I learned was not surprising.

They all knew that criticism was a fact of life that affects all of us almost every day from the time we are born ("Don't touch that—you're bad!") and even after the day we die ("I can't believe that John left so little to his children"). But all of the participants were admittedly confused about criticism and how to give it, take it and give it to themselves. This book will help them, and I hope the rest of us, learn how to employ criticism, so that it enhances our performance and helps us to build more honest and trusting relationships.

CRITICISM IN YOUR LIFE

INTRODUCTION: WHAT IS THIS BOOK ALL ABOUT?

Let's take a quick glance at this book: its intent, its elements, and its value. Chapter 1 focuses on criticism and its power in our lives. It sets the tone for the positive interpretation and utilization of criticism.

Realizing that criticism is inevitable doesn't lessen our desire to think about how wonderful life might be if criticism were eliminated! Chapter 2 captures that fantasy and provides an insight into how things would be different if criticism suddenly were to become illegal. While the chapter may cause you to chuckle, its message is powerful because our very roots as Americans come from our belief in the inherent right to express oneself. Without criticism, we would live in a sterile environment.

Chapter 3 quickly eliminates the fantasy of a world without criticism and introduces you—the receiver of criticism. I've introduced an unusual approach for taking the emotionalism out of criticism. Through the use of the receiver's flowchart, you'll learn how to communicate and interpret the criticism you receive in a way that brings about positive results. The receiver's flowchart enables you to analyze any criticism objectively, sort out the giver's intentions, depersonalize criticism, and assess more accurately whether or not action should be taken. You will be introduced to a step-by-step approach to help you learn how to better utilize the control *you* have as the receiver.

Chapter 4 gives you effective skills for handling the stress produced when you're on the receiving end of criticism. But before you learn how to channel your stress in positive ways, you'll find how to manage that stress better by recognizing many of the factors that produce it. For you, stress may come from the giver's tone of voice, or from the choice of words—recognizing the source of *your* stress also will help you exercise better control. Then, through the use of skills called "Quick Charges" you will be able to positively direct and control your stresses.

Criticism is a double-edged sword. It's not enough for us to receive criticism graciously; we also need to learn how to give criticism effectively. Chapter 5 introduces a flowchart for the giver. This is extremely valuable because it properly prepares you to give criticism effectively. Even though many of us are aware of the importance of being prepared, few of us are effective in practice. Answering each of the questions in the flowchart will ensure that your criticism is appropriate.

Once you're prepared, chapter 6 tells you how to deliver criticism. Building from the findings of a Simmons Market Research Bureau/Bright Enterprises study on criticism commissioned especially for this book, you'll learn the right circumstances for delivering criticism without hurting another's feelings. This is the chapter that explores, for example, what's behind the scenes when coaches yell at their athletes—and the special relationship between them that shares many similarities with all our relationships.

Chapter 7 applies the concepts and skills introduced in previous chapters to specific situations outside the work environment. If you have a problem handling criticism at work, there's a high probability that you'll find it just as difficult at home. Here you'll be introduced to a variety of situations involving criticism among those we love and care about. You'll learn about dealing with the criticism generated from interactions with your children, your mate, your friends, and even that special group from whom our national sample says criticism is most resented—in-laws!

Chapter 8 lets you see through the eyes of others what it's like when you invite criticism. Seeking criticism from others is not something we consciously do, yet many of us unknowingly bring it on ourselves! Observing these "critiholic" styles, you'll better understand others while at the same time avoid setting yourself up.

The old adage that we are our own worst enemies still holds true. It was startling to discover that over 76 percent of the population studied in our survey said that they were extremely hard on themselves. As a result, I've devoted chapter 9 to self-criticism. With practice, you can learn how to take the potentially destructive aspects of self-criticism and use them to enhance your self-growth.

By now it should be evident that handling criticism and the power it possesses is a skill. As with any skill, once you've learned it, you still need to practice. Chapter 10 helps you practice using insights discussed throughout the book. In addition to recapping the key points in the book, there are a few coaching hints to help you get off to a successful start—so that you don't unfairly criticize yourself!

I've included an additional section for you to consider. "On the Firing Line" asks you to think about how you might handle those all-too-common critical situations.

Now, however, we are ready to begin our examination of criticism in all its aspects and from as many points of view as possible. I have chosen to start the journey in an earlier decade, before jumping ahead to a twenty-first-century fantasy world in which an attempt has been made to put an end to criticism once and for all. Let's see what happens.

Chapter 1

THE POWER
OF CRITICISM

The year was 1946. With the Cold War developing rapidly in both East and West, and the idea of détente far in the future, the arrival of that future was not at all certain. The West had already demonstrated its capacity to use atomic weapons and the East was working feverishly on weapons of its own. The place was the Oval Office in the White House:

"Mr. President, I have never been talked to like that in my life."

"Carry out your agreements and you won't get talked to that way."

This exchange of words between Soviet foreign minister V. M. Molotov and President Harry S. Truman was the culmination of a conference in which Truman had unmercifully criticized the Russians for failure to withdraw their armed forces from Poland, as Stalin had agreed to do at Yalta. Throughout the talk, Truman had returned again and again to the same point: Russia had failed to keep her part of the agreement. He was relentless, and, finally, in exasperation, the frustrated Russian diplomat made the above statement—only to find himself, once again, cut down by the pitiless Missourian.

Aside from the fact that his kind of straightforwardness was very much Harry Truman's "style" and the situation had offered a perfect opportunity for him to display it, what was the point in haranguing the Russian minister and, by inference, the Russian government and people as well? Surely they would be displeased with the American chief executive's blatant criticism. What good could come of it?

It seems clear now, with historical hindsight, that President Truman was using criticism to establish firmly the guidelines of a working relationship with the Russians. Like many managers in the business world, he had found himself having to deal with someone else's failure to live up to certain well-defined expectations. Rather than choosing a drastic measure, such as breaking off diplomatic relations, he had sensibly opted to use one of the most powerful forms of communication—stern criticism. In this way, he hoped to make clear that an important part of maintaining a working relationship with *his* company, the United States of America, called for strict adherence to stated agreements, then and in the future. But, most important, he had kept his action within the realm of verbal communication.

History is full of such examples. Some have changed the course of nations, others the future of the world. Consider the Declaration of Independence, for example. Here is an eloquent statement of grievances and intentions, but contained within it, too, is an extensive criticism of George III's management of his American colonies. The purpose of the criticism was to discourage the political and economic association of the colonies with its parent country, England, an act that would be scrutinized by the entire Western world. The verbal communication was directed to the future allies and associates of the new country in an attempt to establish the rightness of its existence, for the American leaders knew that freedom from England would come only with military victory.

The interesting thing about criticism as utilized in the two examples above is that, from the point of view of the giver, it was used for two completely different purposes. In the first case, the response of the receiver of the criticism was crucial. In the second, while the response of the *obvious* receiver was anticipated

and would not change the intent of the giver, the public verbaliza-
tion of the criticism was the essential point. Because criticism is
used for so many purposes and comes in such a variety of guises,
there is no precise way to describe and predict all its functions
relating to human interaction and communication.

One way to get a lively discussion started among your friends is
to introduce the idea that *all* criticism is negative, that concepts
such as "positive criticism" or "constructive criticism" are con-
tradictions in terms. You are almost certain to have some opposi-
tion. But it *is* true! Criticism is, in itself, always negative. "What
about the favorable comments of a music critic?" someone will be
sure to say. "That is positive." Yes, it is—but it is also not criticism. It is praise.

The dictionary tells us that the word "criticism" means the act
of analyzing and making judgments; of finding fault and censuring. "Criticism" derives from the Greek word "*kritikos*," which
comes from another Greek word meaning to discern. So, criticism originally had to do with separating, differentiating. It's
easy to see how differentiating between good and bad falls under
this definition. But there the connection with modern usage
stops. Now, when a statement is made about a literary or artistic
work, it is more correctly called a critique, and is not necessarily
criticism. In fact, when your boss calls you into his office and
tells you what he thinks about your work, he, too, is delivering a
critique. The critique may contain lots of praise (positive comments) or it may contain criticism of your performance (negative
comments). Often, it is these negative comments that remain
with us long after any praise is forgotten. Such is the power of
criticism.

In the following pages, the concept of criticism will be
examined closely so that we may understand how this source
of negative power can be understood, controlled, and used for
constructive purposes. Criticism will be viewed from the per-
spectives of the giver and of the receiver, and from the internal
perspective of giver/receiver when it takes the form of self-
criticism. We will examine ways to deliver criticism so that
desired end results are attained and to face criticism so that it

becomes a valuable learning experience in which you discover more about what you are and what you do. We also will look into ways to become less fearful in both giving and receiving criticism. But before going into these interesting applications of criticism, a few more words are needed to set the stage.

As the receiver we will explore how to face criticism so that it becomes a valuable learning experience. Besides discovering what can be done to enhance performance or better handle future situations, you'll gain insights about yourself. Because participants in the survey said that giving and receiving criticism is equally difficult, we will also look into ways to become more comfortable with either delivering or receiving criticism.

Criticism is negative—always was and always will be! In many respects, criticism functions in the same ways as negative forces in the physical world. It acts to balance out positive forces so that, in ideal situations, equilibrium occurs. When too much or too little of it exists, it can act as a driving force for change in one direction or another. Because criticism is always an available negative force when activated either by ourselves or by others, it can cause dramatic behavioral changes and other potent responses. In this sense, as a kind of force of nature, the power of criticism is neither good nor bad, right or wrong. It is just *there* for us to utilize in the best way we can, as we do with other sources of power available to us.

It was because I recognized the unusual source of power that is contained in criticism that I became interested in developing applications of it for self-enhancement. The way people overlook criticism intrigued me. For eleven years I competed nationally as a platform and springboard diver; for approximately six hours a day a coach would yell, criticizing us continually. I can't recall an athlete ever being destroyed by criticism. Of course, there were times when an athlete would get upset, but no one resented criticism. Quite to the contrary, we knew that as long as the coach was criticizing us, he/she believed in us. Likewise, as a result of conducting workshops nationally, I've discovered that the successful businessmen and women I meet actually seek out criticism from people they respect. They feel that it is necessary because, for them, working in a completely positive environment is like working in a vacuum.

It was also clear to me that despite their recognition of the constructive possibilities of criticism, there existed a great need for having some specific techniques for managing it properly.

In an effort to sort out and identify the ways people use criticism as a positive force, I worked with Simmons Market Research Bureau. Together, we undertook a national study on criticism. In addition to surveying over three hundred people from a variety of businesses, we conducted numerous in-depth interviews. The study explored, among other things, differences between men and women, the types of criticism that hurt the most, when we typically would give criticism, and from whom we most resent receiving criticism.

This book examines the stress that criticism, including self-criticism, produces, and further explores effective ways to channel this stress for constructive purposes.

It's easy to link criticism with stress. In addition to having to deal with the negativity of criticism, there's the stress that is produced by the way it's perceived by others. A manager, for instance, tells an employee that his clothing is inappropriate for an office setting in such a way that the employee interprets the statement as just another complaint from a nitpicking boss. Or a manager uses an unfortunate selection of words and tone of voice in commenting about an employee's work, resulting in the employee's feeling he has been unfairly criticized when, in fact, no criticism was intended. Communication is the problem. If the criticism has been received in this fashion, we want to learn how to develop greater control over the giving and receiving of criticism so that positive outcomes result. It is control that permits this inherently negative force to be directed toward positive channels.

I recall vividly the public criticism that my high school chemistry teacher was so adept at delivering. Because I accepted this criticism as proof of my inadequacy in the subject, I changed my career plans—I never took premed courses in college and never attempted to enter medical school. The criticism this teacher gave was not delivered with the intention of provoking a constructive response in me; it was only belittling and destructive to my self-confidence. Or at least that is the way I reacted to it. If my teacher had another intention in mind, he failed miserably to present it in a way that conveyed his purpose to me. He lacked control in his method of giving criticism and I (now citing my youth as the reason) lacked control in receiving the criticism. The end result, however, was that I reacted to the criticism negatively and changed the direction of my life.

The popular comedian Dom DeLuise was faced with a similar situation early in his show business career. After several months of delivering well-received performances, he was given a number of particularly harsh reviews by the critics. The criticism was so severe that DeLuise lost his confidence and for a time contemplated leaving show business. Fortunately for his fans, he eventually decided that tolerating this sort of criticism was part of the job and he was able to continue in what became a successful career. In this instance, a decision to disregard criticism enabled Dom DeLuise to get on with his life.

Princess Lynn von Furstenberg—who was raised in the South and now lives in New York with her husband, Prince Egon von Furstenberg—told me in a recent interview that as a child of ten she had been criticized strongly for being overweight. She responded by staying in her room and reading a great deal. She also learned to use humor to take the cutting edge off the continual criticism about her weight. Now, as an adult, with all the baby fat long gone, she engages in a regular exercise program to keep herself trim. Not only is she an attractive woman, but she is also an interesting conversationalist and fun to be with. Lynn believes that if she hadn't received all that criticism as a child, she might not have been motivated to develop several important aspects of her personality—she might have grown into a good-looking but boring adult! Here is an instance of someone using strong criticism to empower themselves. Lynn von Furstenberg neither ignored the criticism nor backed away from it. As a young adult, she developed herself, in whatever ways possible, thus making her weight a relatively less important part of the overall impression. In the years that followed, the accumulation of experiences provided Lynn with the insights she needed to address the matter of weight control and overall fitness.

Unfortunately, most people are not aware of how they criticize others—there is little control used and the results are often devastating. This holds true for parents criticizing their children, managers their employees, family members and friends each other, and so on. In part, we have lost our skills in this area of communication. Throughout the late 1970s and early 1980s, it was fashionable to be positive, much the way it was fashionable to be thin. In school, in business, in government, it was important to be a "team player," and that meant going along with the consensus of the group, regardless of what one's personal convictions might be. One was encouraged to take a positive attitude toward things, and criticism was not tolerated. It seems clear that a kind of "group think" was at least partially responsible for some of our more unfortunate scandals of the recent historical past—Watergate and the Iran-*contra* affair being two examples.

It's not that criticism has disappeared over the past twenty-five years. How could it? We're just no longer skillful in giving it and getting it. As a result, it is now often reserved for extreme situations in which the time for constructive solutions to problems has all but passed. The finely controlled art of delivering criticism based on substantial understanding of the receiving individual, drawn from insightful perceptions and specific knowledge about a fellow human being, is simply a rarity now. Similarly, the art of receiving criticism has degenerated into a generalized defensiveness that prevents the receiver from hearing what has been said with an open mind and with insight and understanding of the giver, who is, much more often than not, someone with a vested interest in the success or failure of the receiver.

The interviews I conducted for this book were immensely helpful in revealing just what people were feeling and thinking about the subject of criticism. Most people responded at once to my questions. They apparently felt as though they knew quite a bit about criticism, although many of them only touched the surface of the subject. As I probed further and the interviewees began to relax, statements such as "You know, this is a much more complicated subject than I thought" and "I never paid much attention to how I criticized my kids. Now that I think about it, I could have done a better job" became common.

One professional artist whom I interviewed in New York told me that because artwork is often subject to criticism, she had simply learned not to let other people's criticism of her paintings bother her: "I know that some people will like my paintings and others won't. It would be pretty boring if everybody liked the same things." Laughing nervously, she ended her statement by adding that she had learned that very early in her career as an artist. She learned to separate personal criticism from other types of criticism that are inherent in one's work, as in the case of this particular artist.

Other people defended themselves by denying that criticism ever played an important role in their lives at all. In several of the focus group meetings that I conducted, initial responses to questions about criticism showed that many people felt it had played little or no part in their lives when they were growing up. Few could recall being criticized at any time in their childhood. Many of the group participants even claimed that their friends didn't criticize them now. However, as the meetings progressed and I continued to raise questions, their recollections began to change and on several occasions I found myself, hours later, still being bombarded by specific experiences in which criticism played a major role in an individual's life.

I also observed in conducting these interviews that people tend to refer to criticism as advice if the experience turned out to be positive. "Gee, some of the best advice I ever got was . . ." On the other hand, if the experience was recorded in their mind as being negative, then it is referred to as criticism. Denial of ever being criticized as a child has probably been part of their lives since before the time they had any command of language. A parent's raised voice at a particular behavior pattern and the familiar "No-no" were clearly parental criticism, but interviewees often denied that it was, referring to it as training or guidance. It appears that most people consider criticism to be "bad" in some way: sufficiently so that they attempt to deny their loved ones could have subjected them to it. And that brings us full circle, in a sense, because what this book hopes to show is that while criticism itself may be negative, the ways in which it is used may be good or bad. We wish to focus on how criticism can be used for good, constructive ends, as a powerful, effective communication tool.

Earlier we set self-criticism aside in order to examine criticism as a form of communication between two or more people. In most respects, self-criticism operates in the same way as other forms of communication. All of us have carried on internal dialogues from time to time, examining some issue from more than one point of view simultaneously. We do the same thing when we examine our life situation or our behavior in a particular instance and then critique it. Every time you tell yourself, "I should have said . . . ," "I should have done . . . ," or "Why did I do . . . ?," you are engaged in self-criticism. It is true that we tend to be our own harshest critics. Often what we find tolerable in another person is simply not acceptable in ourselves.

Prolonged, intense self-criticism that is not carefully controlled can have a very damaging effect on our personalities—on our self-confidence and our ability to relate well with other people. All the power of criticism is present in self-criticism. With control, it can become a way to energize ourselves for greater accomplishments—it can lead to the strongest kind of empowerment. Without control, we begin to develop a distorted view of ourselves, lose our balance and perspective on life. When our use of control is faulty, it is generally because we are having trouble sorting out information: separating the true from the false, the real from the unreal. This is when the old adage "This above all: to thine own self be true . . ." could not possibly be better advice.

Chapter 2

CRITICISM: WHO NEEDS IT?

Criticism is not only inherently negative, it can be very hurtful to the receiver as well. Although some people seem to invite criticism into their lives, they hardly ever do it deliberately. Almost everyone has a host of uncomfortable associations related to criticism in one form or another, and most of us want to avoid receiving too much of it.

Criticism probably influences our lives most profoundly when we are children, when we have the fewest resources at our disposal to evaluate the process that is taking place. Even as grown-ups, when we enter into situations in which our role is that of a child, while another's, such as a boss or respected teacher, is that of a critical parent, we can experience the same sort of helplessness that we felt as a child. Our tendency is to revert to our earliest patterns of response when the circumstances we face appear to parallel our deeply embedded experiences. This is most likely to occur when we lack self-confidence or when we feel overwhelmed by the superior power, experience, or knowledge of the other person. It also occurs, of course, when we are aware that the criticism is deserved.

Most of us have felt the damaging effects of criticism, so we may try to keep it out of our lives entirely. When this proves to be

15

impossible, we deny its existence by renaming it and claiming that it is something else. The prevalence of this attitude inspired me to fantasize about a world that was totally devoid of criticism, or almost so. I wondered what life might be like in such a world, what the implications of a society without criticism might be.

A VIEW OF LIFE WITHOUT CRITICISM

Consider a world in which criticism no longer exists, where its practice has been legally eliminated. Let's fast-forward to the mid-twenty-first century for a glimpse of what life might be like under such circumstances before legislation was reversed.

The following excerpt is from the *American World Encyclopedia*, vol. 1 (New York: Gryndl Press, 2035), 437–38.

CRITICISM, Banning of (cont.)
The anticriticism movement began to take shape even before the worldwide political and military upheavals of the mid-1990s. Earlier in that decade, both management and labor had argued for the abolition of performance reviews, declaring them a waste of time and an impediment to productivity. A bill was passed banning these reviews, which became the basis for the more far-reaching Twenty-seventh Amendment to the Constitution, banning the use of all forms of criticism.

By 2004, the Twenty-seventh Amendment had been passed by Congress and ratified by three-fourths of the states, all within two weeks' time (no doubt because most state legislators assumed that criticism of the amendment was in violation of the law), thus making this the fastest passage of a constitutional amendment in the history of the nation to date:

Article Twenty-seven, passed by Congress November 8, 2004.
Beginning immediately upon ratification of this article, the use of criticism by all citizens above the age of sixteen years, for the purpose of censuring, finding fault with, deprecating, degrading, purpose of censuring, finding fault with, deprecating, degrading, belittling, or slandering any other individual or legal entity shall be prohibited.

Until its eventual repeal, in 2032, the Twenty-seventh Amendment was strictly enforced by officers of a congressional crime commission headed by Senator Eliot Momus. Known popularly as "lip busters," the commission apprehended and prosecuted more than fifty-seven thousand offenders during its twenty-eight years of operation. However, by 2025, it had become apparent that the general public no longer favored the law. The proliferation of illegal "speakharshlies" and the widespread sale of underground "critical reviews," which were bringing in estimated net profits of more than $100 billion annually to organized-crime families, had clearly illustrated that critical language could not be suppressed.

When legislation for repeal was presented, it passed in both houses within two hours, with no debate: unanimous ratification of the Thirtieth Amendment, repealing Article Twenty-seven, was completed just four days later.

Many people trace the roots of the ban on criticism back to 1987, when H. Ross Perot, according to an addendum to his contract with General Motors Corporation, had to agree to refrain from publicly criticizing the management at General Motors. A penalty of up to $5 million could be imposed for violation of this agreement.

Gradually, facility with critical language was, for the first time, recognized by the public at large as being an extremely powerful language skill that was not bestowed upon all citizens equally. Those trained in its use, and especially those with a natural "flair" for criticism, were clearly in an advantageous position in many areas of social and business life. Politicians, in particular, were aware that candidates who were adept at using subtle critical language tended to do very well in open debates, while those with less-developed skills invariably ended up less competent. These factors played no small part in establishing the widespread demand for the abolition of criticism in the United States.

Following are a number of newspaper article excerpts and headlines from the period following ratification of the Twenty-seventh Amendment. These provide a capsule insight into the consequences of the new law, as well as public opinion of the time.

Newspaper headline, December 24, 2004:

SUPREME COURT OUTLAWS COLLEGE DEBATE TEAMS

Newspaper article, January 22, 2005:

Buckley, Vidal Convicted!

William Buckley and Gore Vidal were convicted today for violation of New York State laws specifically prohibiting the use of critical language in public forums. The violation dates back to Mr. Buckley's TV broadcast on December 1, 2004, when Mr. Vidal appeared as a guest on the popular talk show "Cutting Corners." The prosecution established that the defendants had engaged in over thirty-two minutes of personal critical exchanges during the course of the program. Superior Court Judge Otton C. Mather carefully avoided direct criticism of the two literary figures in delivering sentence, stating that, hypothetically, "certain corrupters of the youth might well be made an example of, in the future, through public floggings."

Newspaper headline, September 19, 2005:

PRIEST JAILED FOR CONFESSIONAL CHIDING

Newspaper editorial, January 6, 2006:

27th Amendment Devastating

In just over a year since the ratification of the Twenty-seventh Amendment, signs of stagnation and boredom are already evident. In the years to come, we will lose the ability to grow and better ourselves because whatever we do will be accepted with positive approval. Truth will vanish. People will only tell us what we want to hear. Honesty will disappear in our country. Close friendships and deep personal relationships will become a thing of the past because intimate revelation of our true feelings about others has been strictly limited by law.

Newspaper article, May 25, 2006:

Productivity Drop Indicated

The first-quarter P&L reports from leading automobile manufacturers show the lowest level of net profits in over fifty-five years. Spokesmen for the industry unanimously point to reduced productivity as the primary cause of this sharp decline. "Supervisors are unable to point out errors made on the job, and engineers must be satisfied with mediocre results because nobody can comment on shortcomings in anybody's ideas or offer suggestions for improvement," said one vice-president who chooses to remain anonymous. Another high-level manager said that new employees in the workplace are not learning how to build well-rounded work team units because they remain unaware of their weaknesses, do not know how to offset them, and consequently mediocrity has become the norm. This observer was quick to add that his statements were not intended as any sort of criticism but were merely his personal comments on matters of established fact.

Newspaper headline, November 3, 2006:

PROTEST SONGS BANNED FROM TV, RADIO

Newspaper article, March 11, 2008:

China and Glass Sales Reach New High

Industry-wide increases of up to 300 percent in sales have been reported from top manufacturers of china, pottery, and glass. The bonanza sales are attributed to the recent national trend toward smashing dinnerware as a means of expressing anger and relieving stress. A representative for the Cornwall Glass Works said that this tendency is the biggest thing to happen in glass since the stained window craze of the late nineties.

Newspaper headline, February 27, 2009:

KIDS SUE PARENTS FOR $10M—CHARGE WANTON CRITICISM

Jane O'Donnald v. *John O'Donnald*

Jane O'Donnald, the plaintiff, sued her husband, John, for punitive damages resulting from violation of state laws prohibiting criticism in all forms and specifically prohibiting public criticism. The defendant had brought several friends and business associates home to dinner. All details regarding selection and preparation of the food had been left to the plaintiff. The defendant noticed that the guests had barely touched their food and that some of them began leaving much earlier than anticipated.

The defendant then displayed extreme anger and, in front of the remaining guests, loudly berated the plaintiff for being a terrible cook. The plaintiff sought damages for having been personally criticized in public. The court held that the defendant was guilty of two counts of criticism. The defense's claim that Mr. O'Donnald was simply being truthful and honest was overruled as being irrelevant. Because the defendant's criticism of the plaintiff was both demeaning and delivered in public, a fine was imposed and the plaintiff was awarded $3,000.

Lehman, Berman, Doughtery, and Tate, Inc. v. Mary Jones

The plaintiff, a Madison Avenue advertising agency, sued Ms. Jones for damages resulting from self-criticism, citing her behavior as *prima facie* evidence of violation of state laws prohibiting criticism in all forms. After selecting the defendant for employment from a college recruitment program, the plaintiff trained her for over one year at a cost of $30,000. At completion of training, the defendant refused to accept a position as account representative to Whamo Tennis Balls, an important client, stating that she did not feel sufficiently confident to take on such a big responsibility. The defendant also stated that she had carefully considered her poor performance during training and was not certain that a career in advertising was in her best interest. The plaintiff demanded compensation for the cost of training and punitive damages for the embarrassment Ms. Jones's behavior had caused the agency.

The defendant was found guilty on all counts and was remanded to a state institution for six months of indoctrination in noncriticism. She was prohibited from working for any advertising agency for a period of five years and required to pay the plaintiff $10,000 in punitive damages (the court having determined that the cost of training is a normal risk assumed by employers). In delivering the sentence, the judge spoke at length on the dangers of engaging in "this most insidious of all forms of criticism: criticism of self." He continued his comments by saying, "In former times, Ms. Jones, you would have been subjected to shame, ridicule, and public humiliation for this clearly self-indulgent practice. Fortunately, you are now spared that by the very laws that you have violated!"

A RETURN TO REALITY

It is doubtful that in the course of our lifetime or in the foreseeable future criticism will be done away with, legally or otherwise. Our right to criticize others and to be criticized by others will remain intact. In fact, as the dictatorial overtones of some of the examples we've considered suggest, the right to give and receive criticism is a fundamental part of our democratic process. Criticism is just too important to let go of. It brings balance into our lives, provides us with a basis of comparison, and brings meaning to truth, honesty, and intimacy. It enables us to grow and become better at who and what we are, and it helps to keep our egos from getting too big. No, criticism won't go away. In fact, one of the findings from the National High-Tech Management Study that I conducted three years ago was that people actually want it and feel neglected if they are denied it.

In our hypothetical world without criticism, it must have appeared that a lot of unwanted stress had been eliminated from daily life. After all, if you don't have to worry about being criticized, or embarrassed, or about disappointing others, you can avoid a major source of stress and save a lot of energy. And if you don't have to worry about how somebody else will react to your criticism, you can save even more. On the other hand, many people would probably find their lives filled with more stress than ever before, but of a different kind. This is the stress that comes from boredom, the lack of challenge to aspire to higher levels of attainment, or the stress that is produced when you are not able to express your negative feelings about a situation. But there is no point in speculating about hypothetical stress any longer. We have returned to reality, where criticism exists and we *know* that giving it and getting it can be stressful. Later we will discuss how this stress can be directed into positive channels.

In the workplace, criticism seems to be playing an increasingly important role as participative management becomes more and more a reality. Companies are asking employees at all levels to come up with creative ideas, to take risks, and to make speedy decisions. Each of these areas, when practiced, provides a fertile field for criticism. As the business world finds itself drawing away from the enforced "positivism" of the late seventies and the eighties, workers are getting a clear message that what is wanted now is an understanding of their strengths and weaknesses so that the former can be emphasized and the latter minimized by the ways they are managed. The real need to do more with less, to increase productivity while reducing costs, makes this approach essential. And the use of criticism to achieve these ends is more and more recognized as a vital management tool.

There is also a trend toward criticism's playing a greater role in our social lives. At a meeting of corporate public affairs officers in New York City, a speaker named Florence Skelly indicated that "there is a basic hunger to find meaning in life. It approximates a spiritual need or desire and is expressed in a variety of ways, including the placement of more emphasis on formality, the manners and symbols of social acceptability; increased public concepts of personal morality; and a growth in fundamentalist religion." Here, again, are areas of endeavor that are rife with possibilities for criticism. In the hundreds of interviews that I conducted to find out just what the American public actually feels and thinks about criticism, one thought came up over and over again: the recognition that criticism, when properly communicated, helps people to ground themselves, to better understand what they are doing and where they are going. Admittedly, most found it easy to see criticism's applications to their business lives; sufficient numbers were willing to at least admit that criticism probably played a significant role in their personal relationships as well. What is overwhelmingly apparent is the fact that few of us ever really consider the importance criticism plays in influencing our social and professional behavior.

Chapter 3

CRITICISM CLOSE UP: RECEIVING IT

We cannot avoid criticism. It is built into the way we do things: the way we raise our children, the way we conduct business, and the way we establish relationships with others. It simply can't be circumvented. Criticism is experienced by the person who works very hard to avoid it just as frequently as it is experienced by the person who does nothing to avoid it. And once we realize that, we are left with only two clear-cut alternatives: learn some techniques for managing life's criticism and controlling it, or go along giving and receiving criticism in a haphazard manner, often yielding little in the way of constructive development. We will now narrow our focus to look at some of the basic aspects of receiving criticism.

We have said that criticism is a powerful communication tool requiring recognition by both its giver and receiver; that it is *always*, in and of itself, negative; that it exists, of necessity, because it represents the other side of praise and commendation; that our society seems to have lost its skills in utilizing criticism for constructive ends; and that many people look upon it favorably because it plays some important role in self-development. We also recognized that in giving and receiving criticism there exists a great possible source of negative stress. It will be important to

23

keep these background concepts in mind as we explore the ways to develop control, because criticism is potent, complex, and not to be approached in ignorance.

The power of criticism is very real. Just think again about the criticism that you received as a child and the important role it played in determining what you are and what you do today. It is not uncommon for criticism to have been a determining factor in making a career choice, in choosing a particular kind of personal image, or even in selecting a marital partner.

A good example of how the power of criticism might negatively alter the course of a person's life is found in the story of my client Earl. He allowed parental criticism to change his life, and to this day he has been plagued with regrets for having done so. Earl was seriously contemplating marriage to a young woman he had been dating for over two years. His parents, with whom he still lived at that time, had never been enthusiastic about his companion but had never expressed this verbally until Earl mentioned that he was planning to discuss marriage with his girlfriend. The dam burst and a flood of criticism about this young woman poured forth. Convinced that his own feelings and observations were faulty, Earl changed his mind about getting married and soon the relationship became static, faltered, and finally ended. Six months later, having moved out on his own, Earl realized that he had made a mistake and tried to pick up the pieces. But by then the young woman was dating another man, whom she subsequently married. Today, six years later, Earl is unmarried and convinced that he missed out on an important opportunity for happiness in his life because of his decision.

Despite being surrounded by a plethora of such examples, many people still seem to deny the existence of criticism in their lives, especially when it originates with loved ones. The positivism of the seventies and the eighties—the "do and be everything" decades—has encouraged this denial. Some people recognize that criticism is with us but wish that it would magically disappear. It is not very nice and it makes them feel uptight. Well, it *is* here and it won't disappear because it can't, so we might as well take the plunge and begin to explore criticism.

Twelve Points About the Power of Criticism

First of all, let's take a look at what makes criticism so powerful. Here is a list of twelve aspects of criticism, each of which highlights a source of its power.

1. It is a form of communication, rooted in negativity, that attempts to control behavior.
2. Its nature is dependent upon the judgment and intention of the giver.
3. It is interactive.
4. It is eternal. As long as no one is perfect, criticism will exist as part of our daily lives.
5. Its result is dependent upon the perception of the receiver (determined by such factors as the receiver's mood at the time, self-image, and so forth).
6. The criticism giver wants something.
7. The criticism giver assumes that he or she is working from the "right" premise.
8. It points out the negative aspects of behavior, actions, or opinion by using an expression of nonapproval, in an attempt to direct behavior (presumably, for positive end results).
9. It does not always include suggestions for changing or improving behavior.
10. It is given with the expectation that the receiver will change in some way. If change does not occur, there is the implication that a penalty will be imposed.
11. It can be both verbal and nonverbal.
12. Both giving and receiving it is stress-producing.

For the receiver, it's extremely important to keep these twelve points clearly in mind; they are the "givens" of criticism.

Let's expand these points.

If criticism is a method of communication, then, of course, what it communicates is information. And because we are in a technological age in which the transmission of information is crucial in almost every kind of human endeavor, it is assumed that people will be receptive to any information transmitted including criticism. More than anything else, the widespread understanding of the need to communicate accurate information in concise, economical ways has probably set the stage for the need to criticize.

When the difference between success and failure is measured by the narrowest of margins and when the repercussions of the failure of one individual can often be felt throughout an entire organization, the need for direct and economical conveyance of information is absolutely essential.

That there is a need for honest feedback was a significant finding of a National High-Tech Management study, which my company, Bright Enterprises, conducted over two and a half years, and which was later described in my book *Gearing Up for the Fast Lane: New Tools of Management in a High Tech World.*

In-depth interviews revealed that employees wanted to know what they were doing right and what they were doing wrong. The more recent Simmons Market Research Bureau/Bright Enterprises study on criticism further confirmed the presence of this point of view. Respondents said that they *expect* their boss to criticize them. They felt that it's important to give honest feedback because besides improving work quality, it raises confidence levels, instills pride and commitment, and continually renews respect. The key is *honest feedback*—a balance of both praise and criticism.

The receiver's principal task is to depersonalize the criticism and view it as information worthy of objective examination—to see if it is accurate and acceptable, and if it warrants any action. The receiver alone has this control but often fails to utilize it effectively. Because criticism interaction is usually quick and emotionally charged, in order to obtain quality information it is necessary to take a very methodical approach to analysis. In addition, one must remember the conclusions arrived at. This is more difficult than it sounds. Not only do we react to criticism according to habitual patterns of response, when we are being criticized by someone with whom we've had frequent negative encounters—a hostile boss, a rebellious teenager—those earlier encounters may reappear each time we are reconfronted.

THREE STAGES

If it were possible to put emotions aside and freeze each stage of the thinking process we go through when receiving criticism, we would find that we experience an alert stage, an inspection stage, and a motion stage.

The alert stage occurs when we first realize that we are being criticized. There's an internal signal that goes off, alerting our defenses. When it reaches a certain level, we realize we are under attack. The inspection stage includes a further examination of what is being said, how it is being said, the intention associated with the criticism, and so forth. The motion stage is when we accept or reject the criticism and determine whether or not to take action.

We will examine each of these stages in greater detail so that the next time you are criticized, you will be better able to assess your own feelings at any point in the process and also sort out the criticism being delivered. By understanding where you are and what you are feeling as you respond to criticism, you begin to better utilize the control you have as the receiver. By asking yourself certain questions that are relevant to the process, you become an active participant in the exchange, rather than just a passive recipient of criticism.

This methodical approach to dealing with criticism is important for two reasons. First, it assures that you will ask yourself all the important questions about the criticism and its giver: Is the criticism valid? What is the intention behind the criticism? What action needs to be taken?

Second, the very process of going through an established routine helps you to become more objective and less emotional, thereby helping you maintain better control of the situation. Consider a dancer or an athlete who has fallen down while performing, picked himself or herself up, and continued on as though nothing had happened. This ability to overcome feelings and maintain control stems from a methodical approach to learning a routine, from possessing sufficient self-confidence, and from an ability to focus and regain concentration. This is the mark of professionalism. It is something that is particularly applicable to the receiving of criticism, and something that all of us can work at developing in our own lives.

Many of the people I interviewed said that the most disturbing thing about receiving criticism is the feeling that they have lost control and are totally vulnerable to the person giving it. This initial response is not unusual. As we've learned from stress research, each of us is equipped with a primitive fight-or-flight response mechanism. When we feel threatened, our body automatically shifts into a self-defense mode of operating. Many of us have trouble recovering from this natural response, which signifies the first signs of the alert stage. From the beginning, we may remain focused on the emotional aspect of the situation or the hurt feelings engendered by the criticism. As a result, we are unable to gain control over ourselves and over the interaction that is taking place.

Regaining control involves not only becoming familiar with our initial reactions to criticism but also developing a repertoire of skills to reduce the stress and direct it in positive ways. Our positive receptivity to criticism increases when the skills we employ are effective. It's interesting to note that some people who enjoy success in their work and interactions with others usually don't get a lot of practice in receiving criticism. As a result, they don't have many opportunities to develop an effective set of skills.

On the other hand, merely being a frequent recipient of criticism doesn't necessarily ensure that you will be a lot better at dealing with it. Good skills in this area are related to rational thinking and control, and a person overloaded with criticism is often the least able to display these skills.

It seems clear that a wide range of people need to develop skills in receiving criticism. Remember that criticism is simply *information*, and that we color this information with our perceptions, our experiences, and our level of confidence at any given moment. But it is also information that we can clarify, examine, and take control of, to ensure that it is accurate and relevant to our situa-

THE RECEIVER'S FLOWCHART

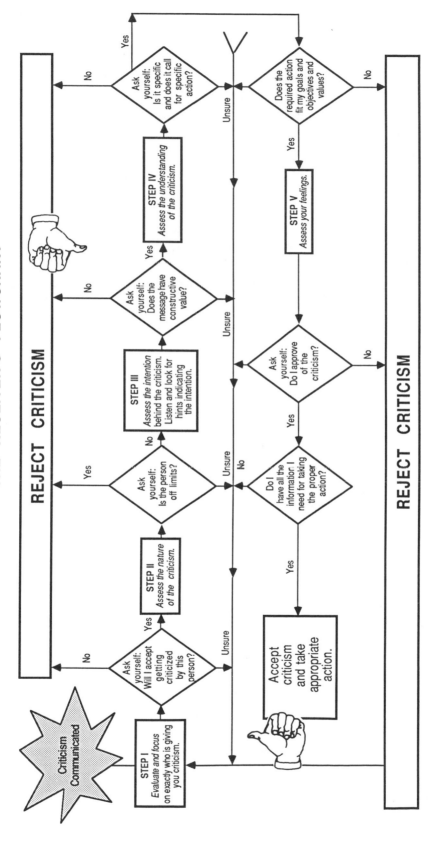

tion. Beginning with this premise, we can learn to reduce our emotional and physical reactions to criticism, enabling us to further explore the source and our interpretation of the criticism.

THE RECEIVER'S FLOWCHART

Step I: Evaluate and Focus

Step I introduces some important questions to keep in mind. Because emotions naturally get aroused at the onset of the criticism process, this signifies the *alert stage*. Here the receiver needs to quickly recover and begin questioning "Who is the giver" and what right do they have to criticize? Is he or she qualified to criticize you? Within bounds in doing so or really off limits? After all, not everybody is in a position to criticize you. All but the smallest children are aware that they are answerable only to certain specific people. Certainly in business and in most other human endeavors, there is an established hierarchy that helps to determine who is in a position to criticize whom. There are good reasons for this—some people have a broader view of a situation, or more knowledge and experience, or have the responsibility for deciding what is acceptable and unacceptable. It is these people who might have the right to criticize those people possessing fewer of these attributes.

Step II: Assess the Nature of the Criticism

Once you have determined that the giver is a person from whom criticism might "legitimately" originate, the next thing to consider is whether or not the criticism itself is within the bounds of your relationship with the giver. If you are unsure, you can always find out by simply asking why the giver believes he or she has the right to criticize. Typical examples of criticism that is out of bounds might include the following: (1) your boss criticizes your wife's style of dress; (2) a neighbor criticizes the condition of your front lawn; (3) a co-worker criticizes your punctuality; (4) a friend criticizes a potential spouse; (5) your parents criticize a car you are planning to buy—with your own money.

If you recognize that the criticism is outside acceptable boundaries—"off limits"—it is a legitimate reason for disregarding the criticism. Because these thought processes occur at lightning speed, we are not always aware of them. It's helpful to be conscious of the person giving criticism, and whether or not that person is off limits, so that you can better interpret the criticism itself.

Step III: Assess Intention

What does the criticizer want? Why are you being criticized? These questions represent the beginning of the *inspection stage.* It's a fact that everybody wants *something,* which is especially true of people who criticize. Your task is to understand the intention of the giver.

It is natural to ask yourself, "Is this criticism intended to place blame on me? To embarrass me? To hurt me? To destroy me? To reject me?" On the other hand, if the criticism is intended to have a constructive end result, the person giving it will want you to understand his or her intent. In fact, a reasonable premise to work from in most cases is that the individual criticizing you is trying to be helpful (unless you have a clear indication that this is not true). After all, if the giver's intention were to hurt you, it would be much more harmful *not* to criticize and let you continue doing what he or she believes to be incorrect!

There are two levels to focus on in any communication: the context, and the subtext, or the material between the lines. This is not a startling or new insight about communication, but one that is important to highlight here. When we are being criticized, emotions often get stirred up, our confidence ebbs, and we tend to misinterpret the message being conveyed. It may take a conscious effort to accurately identify the intention of a criticism.

When considering the context, pay attention to the way the

giver supports the criticism. If he or she defends it or admires it for its own sake instead of for the definite benefits it offers, it's wise to question its purpose.

Two teenage girls overheard on a bus:

TEENAGER #1: Why do you go out with Stan? He's so yucky.
TEENAGER #2: Why do you say he's yucky?
TEENAGER #1: I don't know, you know. He's just kind of, you know . . . yucky.
TEENAGER #2: That doesn't tell me anything!
TEENAGER #1: Okay. He never says hi to me.

In this case, Teenager #2 got a quality insight on what inspired criticism of Stan. Listening to the subtext of words will reveal valuable information about the intention behind criticism.

Words are not only communication tools, they can be stress triggers as well. This is especially true when criticism is involved. When I was a child, for example, if I was bad, I suddenly became "Deborah," no longer the cute, friendly "Debbie." Hearing myself called "Deborah" was generally enough to create a substantial level of stress within me. Similarly, certain phrases, such as "you should have" or "you must," cause many people to feel they are being addressed as if they were children. This brings out associated feelings of stress and of being out of control. Other specific words, such as "always" and "never," also have been shown to be stress producers. One marketing executive whom I know says he absolutely can't stand it when his boss says, "You *never* seem to do [such and such] the way I want it." The use of the word "never" in such contexts angers him to the point where objectivity and control are greatly diminished.

Nevertheless, considering the words used, capturing the meanings behind them and expanding upon those meanings, is a reliable way of "sorting out" the intentions of someone who is criticizing you. After all, if you assume that the criticizer wants something, it is reasonable also to assume that clues to what they want will be contained in the words they use, even if not directly revealed through the context of their language.

When, for instance, a person says, "You look great today," you wonder what that means about the way you looked on other days. Similarly, when someone says, "Let me be totally honest with you," you think that perhaps on other occasions he or she has been less than honest.

Then there's the person who says, "I don't mean to criticize but . . ." and you know that the criticism is coming.

To help reveal the full meaning contained in the criticism, scan the situation. This involves listening to the message while at the same time focusing on the big picture. One method is to ask yourself, "Where is this person coming from?" Review what you know about his or her own problems and frustrations. What is their true position in this matter likely to be? Often, this deliberate combining of a macro- and a micro-focus leads to a moment of revelation in which the real meaning behind the criticizer's words becomes clear to you.

A good example of this is the recent experience of the wife of one of my clients. Charles is a successful ad agency executive who squandered much of his youth in fruitless pursuits and is now, in his own words, "making up for lost time." Charles is not only very self-critical, he is also very critical of his wife, Joy—a practice that almost always draws a negative response from her. When Charles said to her not long ago, "It really bothers me when you waste a lot of time like this," rather than just becoming upset, as usual, Joy stopped and asked herself, "Where is Charles coming from?" Suddenly she was able to see beyond the words Charles was using; it was clear to her that what Charles was criticizing her for were those characteristics that he most disliked in himself. He was simply projecting some of his self-criticism onto her. Joy recalled that Charles frequently apologized immediately after criticizing her, indicating that his words were really not intended for her. With this understanding, Joy now feels she has some control over the situation and is no longer as troubled by the criticism. Although not an excuse for Charles's behavior, it does help explain it. This kind of situation is similar to the common practice of being severely critical of family and friends after a particularly difficult day at work. The criticism is really intended for the circumstances the giver finds himself or herself in, or for those responsible for creating the situation. It is, however, delivered to whoever is around to hear it.

As you try to ascertain intention, watch verbal and nonverbal changes in the individual's behavior or physical state while speaking. These include the critic's sudden need for a glass of water or a drink when speaking about certain subjects; nervous darting of the eyes, back and forth, or the inability to look at you directly; changes in tone of voice when specific words and phrases are used or when he or she is talking about a certain topic; and jerky movements of facial muscles or hands in the same circumstances.

Even the person's voice quality reveals a great deal. Suzette Haden Elgin, in her book *The Gentle Art of Verbal Self-Defense*, says that voice quality is affected by, among other things, stress. When stress levels increase, there is a higher pitch or greater volume, or both. Thus, a helpful intention can easily become masked by a harsh voice quality.

These clues are most difficult to interpret and doing so calls for substantial experience on the part of the interpreter. However, if you know the person involved and have had many interactions with him or her, you will have a basis of normal behavior from which to make comparisons. When the giver has intentions that are different from the message that his words convey, he will speak and react differently than usual, unless he is very adept at maintaining a "poker face." In that case, your own experience may be insufficient, by itself, to penetrate this person's word ciphers, and more subjective approaches will probably yield better results.

Verbal and nonverbal inputs can powerfully influence one's intuition. There are many internal clues that will let you know that your intuition is at work. Some of these are related to the way in which we access information in our brains. Some people tend to deal with information visually, others auditorially, and still others by way of touch, or kinesthetically. So when you begin to "see" just what a person means, or really "hear" what he or she is saying, or begin to have a "feel" for what is going on, you should pay close attention to what your unconscious mind is giving you—your intuition is at work! As a Chicago doctor said to me, "I can't always put my finger on exactly how I know when someone's intention is constructive or not. But I can sense it and experience has shown me that I am almost always correct in my feelings." The doctor is apparently a kinesthetic type (not a bad thing in a medical person), as is evidenced by his use of the phrase "put my finger on" something—to literally touch it—and speaking of being correct in his "feelings." He has also learned to rely on his intuitive responses—something that the best diagnosticians work at developing.

If your intuition is developed, it is probably your most reliable tool in assessing another person's intentions. It amounts to giving voice to a preconscious thought process. Your intuition represents a response to a composite of all the subliminal cues that the giver has been unable to shield from you.

Step IV: Assess Understanding

However, if you are still unsure about the giver's intention, it is never too late to ask him. Is this criticism specific? Does it call for specific action? Direct your energy toward making sure that you understand the literal content of the criticism. If someone said to you, "Your presentation was boring, it gave no new insights, and we thought you were not prepared!," you would be faced with criticism that is highly charged emotionally, yet in other respects quite weak. It is not specific about what you did wrong, and it gives no indication of what is wanted instead. Remember in receiving criticism, *you* have control. Part of that control is in your ability to inspect the information that is being given to you.

Inspection of criticism focuses on whether or not its content is specific. Most of us are aware of this, but it's only easily recalled later, at a time when our emotions are under control. When our stress level rises, we have a tendency to forget such obvious things. If the information we receive is about ourselves, we too frequently accept it as truthful and bypass the inspection stage. That's why it's valuable to maintain perspective: criticism is simply information and thereupon open to our scrutiny. After all, we regularly scrutinize other information we hear, and we seldom balk at questioning its reliability.

As has previously been pointed out, criticism need not contain suggestions for changing or improving behavior, although it *might*. What good criticism must do is convey to you, very specifically, what is wrong and what is wanted instead. This is what constitutes the transmittal of good information, the *raison d'être* for criticism in the first place. If you find in the course of your inspection that you are not obtaining this kind of information, clarify what the desired change is. Otherwise, you run the risk of making changes that lead only to more criticism. It's what I call the "criticism spiral."

A friend of mine, Ron, could easily describe what it's like to be caught up in the criticism spiral. Ron worked as an administrator for a large state university system for many years and told me of the tension he worked under for most of the time he was there. His boss loved to criticize; he seemed to extract particular delight in seeking out and finding new areas that he could criticize. No matter was too small to escape his attention. He was masterful at specifically identifying things he didn't like—there was never any doubt left in any employee's mind about that. What he regularly failed to do, knowingly or otherwise, was to be the least bit specific about the way he wanted things to be done. As a result, changes were continually being made in response to his criticism, more often than not opening up ever-increasing new fields for more criticism. Ron was thoroughly frustrated. "If I knew then what I know now, I would have been sure to ask for specifics and put an end to his game."

When criticism is properly presented, there is no doubt as to what is expected in the future: "Harry, when you closed that deal with the Acme Corporation, you promised a two-week delivery date for the widgets. Company policy is never to promise delivery in less than thirty days unless the assistant vice-president gives written approval. In the future, please stick to that policy."

It's not likely that criticism will fail to identify the action, attitude, or occurrence that its giver is dissatisfied with. This would make it all but pointless. But it is quite possible that the expected change is left unspecified or ambiguous. Remember to inspect criticism for specificity, not only for what you are doing incorrectly but also for the changes that are being expected of you.

If you continually find there is a lack of specificity in the criticism itself, or in the action desired by the giver, you might want to consider seriously rejecting the criticism. Without knowing exactly what is wanted of you, it is impossible to determine whether the changes you intend to make will be the right ones, compatible with the goals and objectives that you and others may have established.

Also consider whether the criticism fits into your own goals and objectives. If it does not, are you willing to alter those goals and objectives? Just how firm are they?

June had worked for Jim for approximately two years and they had developed great mutual respect for one another. Jim believed June could move into the corporate suite if she wanted to—which she did at the onset. He helped by putting her in situations in which she would be more visible. Initially, she handled herself professionally. However, as time went by, he could see that she tended to make comments that were inappropriate, and that she was becoming frustrated. During lunch one day, he told her that her problem was that she was not well informed enough. He pointed out to her that many decisions were made after five o'clock; if she wanted to know what was really going on and get down in the trenches with the real powers in the organization, she needed to join them after work. Jim was careful not to suggest to June that it was necessary to match the big boys drink for drink, but just that she needed to spend some time with the "guys." She viewed his comments as a criticism, and, after a period of deliberation, decided that if she had to do that to be promoted, it simply wasn't worth it. She changed her career goal.

Step V: Assess Your Feelings

Consider your emotional/rational response to the criticism. Do you approve of the criticism? Do you approve of the way it is being given? It is important to recognize that you exercise the greatest control when making these kinds of determinations. Even criticism that is backed up by documentation and specific examples may not take all of the facts into account and may therefore be unjustified. Deciding whether you approve of the criticism and are willing to take action makes up the *motion stage*. Determining the accuracy and merit of the criticism is a difficult decision in the acceptance process. The more honest you can be with yourself, the better your decision will be. It is also important to remember that this determination should only be made after you have considered the validity and intent of the giver (Steps I–III). Having decided that the giver is qualified to deliver criticism and that the intent is for some constructive purpose (or that you are willing to temporarily disregard the purpose), then you will be psychologically prepared to make an honest objective decision as to whether or not you agree with it.

Acceptance of the actual language and technique of delivery that the giver employs is equally important. A common goal between the giver and receiver can ease the way for such acceptance. When two people who work together or interact on a regular basis know what is wanted by each other and how the other is capable of performing, it is possible to develop realistic expectations about each other's behavior. Over time, a solid foundation of mutually shared expectations supports a relationship based on confidence, trust, and respect.

When the giver and receiver of criticism have a good working relationship—that is, a relationship built on high levels of personal and professional acceptance and mutuality of goals—then it becomes easier for the giver to present criticism and for the receiver to accept and utilize it. Many questions become irrelevant in such cases; the receiver accepts that the giver has a right to criticize and that the intention, whether immediately identified or not, is meant to effect a positive end result. Ironically, the receiver pays little attention to how the criticism is delivered. Instead, attention is focused on the relevance of the criticism and the value to be gained. But when the opposite is true, tolerance for language and delivery technique may be low regardless of the honesty associated with the words being spoken. You may decide to reject the criticism because its presentation is unacceptable. There are exceptions, as might be expected. Certain factors may exist that suggest it's far better to focus on the acceptance of the criticism and the content being delivered—when the criticism comes from the president of your company, for instance.

Even if the president has a gruff voice, a tendency to speak loudly, and is somewhat lacking in tact and sensitivity, common sense reminds you that rejection of criticism from the president might lead to a variety of unpleasant penalties. A sensible approach to this kind of situation would be to reframe your thinking about what is acceptable in receiving criticism. Your nonapproval of the method of its delivery is of little importance; you must reject the president's delivery technique while still hearing his message, which may be of substantial value to you. This also improves your chances of being able to employ what you have learned here at some future time with the same company!

The important thing to remember is that when you arrive at answers to the questions "Do I accept this criticism as relevant and accurate? [Is the information good or not?]" and "Do I approve of the way it is being given?," you are preparing the way to exercise control over the interaction by accepting or rejecting the criticism that is being presented. This decision should only be made when enough "cooling off" time has elapsed and you are certain that a proper balance of emotional and rational input is available to base the decision on.

Recheck Your Information

The final question you must ask yourself before deciding to accept the criticism is whether or not you have all the information you need to take proper action. If you have any doubt about this, review the questions you previously considered to see if there is any further information to be gleaned in these areas. You might also wish to obtain further clarification from the giver of the criticism, if appropriate, by asking direct questions. When you are satisfied that you possess all the information you need, you have arrived at the point of taking appropriate action. The journey is over and you will find that you feel a greater sense of inner strength, so that next time you travel this path, it will be easier.

Chapter 4

HELP IN HANDLING CRITICISM

Eleanor Roosevelt once observed, "No one can make you feel inferior without your consent." Let's see how well this quote applies to you as a receiver of criticism. I'll ask you some questions; your answers should reflect the way you typically react.

1. Do you tend to assume automatically that the person criticizing you is correct?
2. Do you quickly become defensive when someone criticizes you?
3. Do you tend to stop listening when someone is criticizing you?
4. Do you start crying?
5. Do you become argumentative?
6. Do you take criticism from others personally?
7. Do you deny your mistake and place the blame on others?
8. Do you start yelling?
9. Do you ask questions in an effort to make the criticism clearer and more specific?
10. Do you ask questions to sort out the intention of the criticism?
11. Do you quickly want to move from the criticism to finding out ways to rectify the situation?
12. Do you take steps to ensure that you are not being personally rejected?

There are no right or wrong answers to any of these questions. What's important is to take the time to become more aware of how you respond to criticism.

In our national study, we asked participants the same set of questions. You may find that your answers closely resemble theirs. For instance, respondents stated that they most frequently react to criticism by:

1. Taking it personally (especially women), regardless of whether the criticism comes from parent, in-law, mate, boss, or child.
2. Becoming defensive; particularly true of criticism from parents.
3. Asking questions to make the criticism clearer and more specific; most frequently regarding criticism from a boss, co-workers, subordinates, children, and, surprisingly, from a spouse.

As you are probably all too painfully aware, it's tough to receive criticism. But you might find it encouraging to learn that the *receiver* has more control than the *giver*. As a result of reading through the Receiver's Flowchart in chapter 3, you should realize that it's the receiver who has more control than does the giver. For some of you, this may come as a surprise; however, the giver's control lies only in the initial phase of the criticism process. (We will discuss the giver and the initial or preparation phase in more detail in chapter 6.) Once the criticism is communicated, it's the *receiver* who decides whether the criticism is within limits, whether it's valid or can be supported by specific examples, and whether it's worthy of acting on. Of course, if the giver is in a position of authority, control can revert back to him or her if the receiver takes inadequate or inappropriate action.

Being aware of the inherent control the receiver has will enable us to take the potentially negative effects of criticism and redirect them in more constructive ways. It is not necessary to learn how to take control, because, as receivers, we already have it! But most of us fail to recognize this fact and are at best able to capture only the illusion of control. Before we discuss how to make the most of our control, though, let's talk briefly about what control really is.

WHAT IS CONTROL?

Control might be defined as maintaining flexibility while keeping a proper focus in order to achieve specific short-term and long-term goals. Many of us, unfortunately, misperceive what control is and equate it with inflexibility. This is especially true of successful people who are used to getting things accomplished by doing them in a certain way. They not only want to take control over the end result, they also want control over the means by which it is accomplished.

This type of person is less open to different ways of achieving a particular goal. We all know people like this. Are they in control? They might have been once, but now they are inflexible. There's only one way to get anything done, these people assert, and that's "my way."

People also try to create an aura of control by imposing external restrictions such as strict schedules and routines. "If I read for twenty minutes a day, exercise continuously for thirty to forty minutes a day, block my calls at work, then I'll be in control," they may tell themselves. "Coffee in the morning with my paper, blue suit for big meetings, and out of the house by seven-twenty-five." You may be thinking that this intense scheduling is a sign of good organization. That is true, but our attempts to organize ourselves to gain greater control may unwittingly cause us to become inflexible. This shows up in the way a person reacts when things don't go as planned. The inflexible person gets upset, whereas the person in control quickly recovers and moves on.

Philip, the CEO of a large Chicago-based telecommunications company, gets up very early in the morning, when it's usually still dark outside. To avoid waking his wife, he dresses in the dark. In order to facilitate dressing, Philip places all his socks strategically in his drawer according to color. His shirts and suits are lined up in his closet according to style and color. In the morning, his "game" is to put on his clothes quickly without having to turn on any lights. Is he organized? Yes. His system is highly efficient. However, when someone, probably his wife, puts his clothes away in the wrong place, he becomes *extremely* agitated. It's not simply an inconvenience or a temporary setback, it's a disaster of catastrophic proportions. Philip is no longer in control. Philip is *inflexible*.

Here's a quick and simple test to examine whether you are in control or whether you tend to be inflexible.

1. Do you have to sleep a certain number of hours at night? If you don't get this amount of sleep, are you sluggish the next day?

2. Do you have to drink a cup of coffee in the morning to wake up?

3. Do you have to read the newspaper in the morning? If you don't see the paper, do you feel out of touch all day?

4. Do you view yourself as an evening (or a morning) person? If you think of yourself as a night (or a daytime) person, are you concerned about your ability to be effective if an early-morning (or late-afternoon) top-level meeting is planned?

5. Do you organize your personal belongings in a certain way in your closets or drawers? If someone disturbs your system, do you get upset?

6. If you don't exercise at the same time every day, do you feel out of sorts?

7. If a meeting or an appointment is canceled at the last minute, do you become irritated and have a difficult time adjusting?

8. Do you have to shower before going to bed? If you don't shower, do you have trouble sleeping?

9. Do you have to sleep on one particular side of the bed? If you have to sleep on the other side, do you get annoyed and even have a hard time falling asleep?

10. If you present a particular idea, are you receptive to changing your viewpoint if others disagree?

If you answered yes to more than half these questions, you're in danger of becoming inflexible. These questions are by no means conclusive, but they are indicative of your degree of adaptability.

Developing greater control means becoming more flexible.

When we are in control and flexible, it is easier to bounce back after receiving criticism and keep ourselves focused on the desired end result. We are better able to deal with our emotions so that feelings of disappointment and anger won't rob us of the precious energy we need to achieve specific goals. When we are in control and flexible, we can see the macro-picture even though we are involved in the micro-picture.

When we are on the receiving end of the criticism process, it's important that we effectively use the control that being the receiver gives us.

Let's explore what this means.

Confidence: The Foundation

At the root of establishing greater control and handling criticism is the psychological foundation of confidence. Self-confidence is what we need to spur us into action. It's a demonstrated faith in one's abilities, skills, and characteristics. Self-confidence is the ability to tell ourselves, "I know from past experience that I have what it takes to complete a particular task or goal." As one corporate manager told me, "Confidence is the feeling you have before getting all the facts."

Confidence better enables us to handle criticism from others because we are not as easily threatened. We are able to listen to what the giver has to say without taking it personally, and we can more accurately evaluate what is being said.

As Suzi Jaffe, president of S.D.J. Associates, a successful venture capital firm, told me, "When you are sure of who you are and what you are doing, you respond in a like fashion to the person giving you the criticism, regardless of his or her level. You know you are performing a function and fulfilling a role and that being criticized is something you learn to take professionally instead of personally. Criticism is interpreted as simply one of the costs of doing business."

Howard Mase, organizational development specialist for a major bank, agrees: "The greater your self-confidence, the easier

it is to respond well to criticism." An excellent example of someone who exudes self-confidence is Lt. Col. Oliver North, the key
witness in the congressional Iran-*contra* hearings in the summer
of 1987. Colonel North maintained his control during several
days before the congressional investigating committee and the
nation, even though he was subjected to the severest criticism for
his attitudes and behavior during the time he functioned as operations director for the National Security Council. Colonel North
answered the committee's questions with such an air of cool
confidence and apparently forthright conviction that he even
impressed many of his detractors.

Confidence doesn't come naturally to most of us; it is something we learn. But how do you become more confident?

Fortunately, my diving coach forced me to think about this
question years ago. After a frustrating workout in West Palm
Beach, Florida, I emerged from the pool with tears in my eyes. My
coach came over and put her arms around me and whispered in
my ear, "Debbie, you can be a champion. Everything is there—all
you need to do is believe in yourself and be more confident."

As soon as her words sank in, I got goose bumps. "Somebody
believes in me," I said to myself. At the same time, a lump formed
in my throat, though I wondered how I could become confident.
After years of asking myself and others this question, I've discovered only three ways to build self-confidence.

Before you read these three premises, take some time to write
down on a sheet of paper all your strengths. Now think about the
criteria you used when determining those strengths. Perhaps you
based your list on what people have told you, or on your own
experience. This leads us to our first premise.

Premise I: Knowledge

The more you know about something, the more confident you
feel. Experience adds to that knowledge base. Remember when
you first learned how to drive a car. You gripped the steering
wheel with both hands. Then one day you realized you could lift

one hand off the wheel to wave at a friend. Your feelings of competence got a real boost. Or remember your insecurity when you started working at your first job. As time passed and you learned your job, those uncomfortable feelings vanished and you knew your way around the office like a veteran. Knowledge is the first step.

Premise II: Success

Building a solid knowledge base without putting it into action and experiencing some success does little to further self-confidence. Whenever we engage in various life experiences, each of us needs a certain amount of success—a promotion, say, or a merit raise—in order to build our confidence.

Premise III: Control

Finally, in order to enhance our self-confidence, we need control. This has two dimensions. First, control relates to having a sort of "hands-on" experience with a particular project, so that when it is successfully completed, the person can attribute the success to himself or herself.

An example that I frequently use in workshops to illustrate this point involves Angela, a five-year-old girl, and her mother. Angela is watching her mother bake a cake. It's her first time in the kitchen.

When the cake is finally finished, with the last drop of frosting in place, the mother proudly says, "Angela, look what you did, sweetheart. It's beautiful—you did such a good job." Angela blushes as she tucks her chin into her chest and looks at her mother and says, "Oh, Mom, I didn't do it, you did." She is right; her mother did just about everything. In order for Angela to interpret the success as her own, or to at least share in the success, she needs to be more involved in the project and complete certain steps on her own.

The second aspect of control is knowing the specific steps that lead to the successful completion of a particular project or task. Having this type of control is extremely valuable because, as we all know, once you've been successful, it's important to be able to repeat the success time and time again. If we are not aware of what we specifically did to make our success possible, it's frightening to know that we have to repeat it.

Discussing each of these factors is important because any one factor, or a combination of these factors, will affect the way we perceive and respond to criticism.

ASSESSING YOURSELF

Using the three premises—knowledge, success, and control—as a base helps to answer the question, How do you become confident? To understand how to build self-confidence—and our ability to handle criticism—it's important to discuss: (1) recognizing and interpreting our reactions to situations; (2) identifying personal strengths and weaknesses; (3) being aware of our internal "dialogue"; and (4) understanding how we define success and failure for ourselves.

Recognizing Our Reactions

Assessing ourselves in a particular situation involves processing what we know about ourselves to determine whether or not we are functioning at our best. At the same time, we need to see how our reactions are affecting the situation. When I talk about optimal performance levels, most people whom I work with are surprisingly unaware of specific internal signs that indicate they are at their best. They are, however, readily able to detect the signs of *not* being at their best. A good question to raise is: How can you feel good about yourself if you don't know what it feels like?

Take a moment to write down the answers to the following questions:

1. How do you know when you are at your best?
2. What are the signs?

Each of us has an optimal performance level. When we are at that level, our ability to handle situations—including those in which we are being criticized—is increased. Many of us look for that optimal level when we give ourselves a final glance in the mirror just prior to going to work or before we answer an important call or give a presentation. We all check for a number of signals that indicate to us that we are ready for action.

Don't be surprised if you had difficulty coming up with specific signs. As I mentioned, many people don't pay attention to their reactions. Most of us have been encouraged to focus on what we *do* throughout the day rather than what we think or feel. As a result, when a stress-producing situation arises, it's easy to lose control of ourselves and our ability to deal with the situation effectively.

In essence, it's important to learn how to recognize those times when we are functioning at our peak, and, conversely, when we are not.

For example, when we recognize that we are not at our best, we know that it won't take much to cause us to lose control. When we feel down, we are more likely to accept the validity of the criticism we receive from others. After all, it fits in with the low self-esteem we are experiencing at the moment.

When our repertoire contains effective "self-adjusting skills," we are better able to compensate for a bad mood, impatience, and so on, and stay at or near our best even when we don't feel in top form.

Interpreting Our Reactions

When interpreting information about yourself, it's extremely important to avoid *judging* your reactions. The reactions we have are not right or wrong. They either help or hinder in the achievement of various goals, and we should think about them objectively in this light: Do they bring us closer to achieving our goals, or do they lead us farther away?

Here are two examples that will make this point clear. Both involve playing with coins in your pocket. In the first incident, this reaction will help you achieve *more* of what you want; in the second, it will help you achieve *less* of what you want.

First incident: You are on the board of directors of a local arts center, and the board is presently meeting to decide which of two paintings to buy. You dislike both choices intensely, but your colleagues outvoted you at the last meeting. You know that if you say anything now it will be inappropriate and may cause you to lose your composure. So, to keep yourself under control while sitting in your conference chair, you bury your hands in your pockets and fiddle with the coins.

Second incident: You are about to make a presentation to the board about your committee's activities. As you begin speaking, to help overcome a feeling of awkwardness, you place your hands in your pockets and start idly playing with your change.

Is it "wrong" to stick your hands in your pockets when speaking? No; but it makes you less effective because you are creating a distraction for your audience. Chances are great that when the audience is directing their attention to what's going on inside your pockets, they are missing what you are saying.

For another example that suggests reactions may be neither right nor wrong, good nor bad, consider parents who have two or more children. Ask them if they can treat each child exactly the same to get a similar result. The answer will almost always be a resounding no! What works for one person may not work for someone else. Because of these differences among people, your focus should be on reacting in ways that will help you attain your goal.

Another guideline to keep in mind when interpreting information *about* yourself is to look for changes *in* yourself. It's helpful to recognize such changes because then you will be better able to detect when you are moving outside your optimal range. By using the appropriate skills, you can regain control of yourself quickly.

Consider the situation of Andrew, who learned to control his temper by paying greater attention to his own reactions in various situations. This has been particularly helpful at the regularly scheduled Wednesday-morning interdepartmental meetings. Laura, one of the managers who is present regularly at the meetings, has always annoyed Andrew. Laura talks slowly and deliberately, and takes forever to make her point. This alone strains Andrew's patience, but when she makes a fuss about an insignificant issue and indirectly blames Andrew for it, he loses control. Andrew has been known to shout, slam his fist on the conference room table, and storm out of the meeting, refusing to deal with what he perceives to be ridiculous accusations. As a result, Andrew was acquiring a reputation for being a "hothead" who can't handle criticism.

Now, when Andrew goes to these Wednesday-morning meetings, he's better able to control himself. When Laura directs her criticism at him, he's able to recognize quickly when his stress level is near the boiling point. Instead of blowing his cool, Andrew has taught himself some skills to use instantly in situations to reduce his stress and regain control. These skills are called "quick charges." We will talk about them in more detail later in this chapter.

For Andrew, combining his knowledge about his internal performance signals with his goal—desiring to be more levelheaded at meetings—enabled him to assess his overall effectiveness readily and progress toward achieving his goal. As a result, Andrew now can choose to avoid confrontation if he so wishes.

Knowing Your Strengths and Weaknesses

Intrinsic in building confidence is knowing our strengths and weaknesses. For when we have this understanding, our confidence isn't shaken so easily. We are better able to control our reactions because we are less apt to be caught by surprise.

Furthermore, having an awareness of our strengths and weaknesses helps us to know how to best approach various situations.

Theresa's case is a good example. She is a department head who was asked at the last minute to make a short presentation about her group's progress at an upcoming meeting. Theresa is not very good at giving presentations, primarily because she gets extremely nervous in front of an audience. As a result, her speeches sound flat. She knows that her poor delivery would take away from delivering an upbeat description of the department's recent success.

Theresa decided that, rather than give the presentation herself, she would ask Jane to fill in. Jane is one of her subordinates who is at ease giving presentations to large groups and is extremely effective. Her decision to let Jane give the presentation resulted in a happier ending. Jane was exposed to other department heads and was extremely proud of her performance. Theresa's department, because of Jane, gave the best presentation.

Inner Thoughts

To develop greater control and self-confidence, you need to become more aware of your inner thoughts, especially when you are involved in uncomfortable situations. When you are being criticized, it's easy to slip into thinking about what plausible excuses you can come up with to justify your poor performance. Instead, pay attention to what is being said—and what you are thinking. When you fail to focus on exactly what's being said, you're apt to defend yourself in an inappropriate way.

Among the most interesting results of the Simmons Market Research Bureau/Bright Enterprises study, in which people from ages twenty-five to fifty-five-plus were surveyed, was finding out what thoughts race through people's minds when they are being criticized. First, we explored what people think when their boss is criticizing them. Many of their thoughts were found to be directed either outwardly toward the boss or inwardly toward themselves.

Your inner thoughts may go something like this:

- "Here we go again, if only he'd see the point."
- "I want to defend myself, but I've been with the company six years and I don't want to leave. I'll just keep my mouth shut; she may move on to something else."
- "He's right; I'm wrong."
- "Oh, no, what did I do now?"
- "How much does he know about the subject?"
- "Is she right, or is she being picky?"
- "I feel ashamed and angry at myself for not being worthy of praise."
- "I have let him down, and I don't want it to happen again."
- "Is he right? Have I failed? Could I have avoided this situation?"

However, inner thoughts may be directed toward scrutinizing the criticism further. For instance, respondents in the study also said:

- "This problem is considered important to management—it requires early correction."
- "Is this criticism legitimate?"
- "Is it valid?"
- "Is it constructive, or is she doing it to boost her own ego?"
- "What degree of importance is he placing on the criticism? Is it really no big deal, or is he forming a lasting impression?"

A third group of thoughts revolves around the consequences of the criticism, as in "I'm getting a poor evaluation, so my raise probably won't be as much as I was counting on. And I worked harder than I ever had before. . . ."

By far the most common inner thought when receiving criticism from the boss is taking the criticism personally.

It's precisely at this moment that you'll want to keep criticism in proper perspective, and calm yourself by making sure that your breathing remains smooth and regular. We will talk about how to do that more in depth later in the chapter.

To gain better control of your thoughts, it's helpful to remind yourself to view the comments as information. Try not to make snap judgments about the boss and don't immediately personalize what he or she is saying. Also avoid labeling what is being said as either right or wrong—otherwise, you might find yourself engaged in a competitive match that may result in winning the battle but losing the war.

Remaining impartial enables you to perceive what is being said more accurately and objectively. It also makes it possible to really capture the message that the giver of criticism is communicating. At the same time, you'll want to direct your energies toward controlling your thoughts. As one respondent noted: "It's basically hearing out someone else's side of the story. The other person, whether it be your boss, or your partner, may not be totally right, but it's helpful to hear the person out and consider what he or she is saying, realizing that the person is coming from the premise of being right."

So far we've concentrated on criticism from a boss. But do similar thoughts cross our minds when our mates criticize us? We asked this probing question of our respondents and most of them acknowledged that they think similar thoughts when their mates are criticizing them as when their bosses are criticizing them. What is surprising about the finding is that both the bosses and the mates create similar reactions in our respondents.

One woman elaborated further on the survey form and said, "As with my boss, I evaluate if it's just [my husband's] own opinion or if it's a criticism that has value and is important to my personal or professional growth." Another respondent observed, "I view the criticism more seriously when it comes from my spouse."

The minority of interviewees who said they deal differently with criticism from boss and from mate reported a whole range of reasons. One respondent who reacted differently with criticism from boss and from mate had this to say: "With the boss, what typically goes through my mind is 'The mistake got to this unfortunate point. How can I avoid it in the future?' But with my wife, it's not the same because my wife is highly critical of everything. Therefore, I generally ignore her." Another respondent said that the difference lies in the fact that her boss can fire her, while her husband can't. Furthermore, she said, "Criticism from my husband is very rare, and when it does come, unlike criticism from my boss, it is given very tactfully." A third interviewee gave a similar explanation, saying, "My partner knows me very well and usually criticizes at the right time."

Whether the criticism comes from our boss, partner, children, friends, parents, or in-laws, we color it with our thoughts and feelings about ourselves, the other person, and the issue at hand. Our thoughts in certain situations can impair our ability to hear accurately. Thoughts are also linked to self-fulfilling prophecies. Some medical experts believe our thoughts are closely connected to our health, our emotions, and our perception of various situations. Positive thinking helps us to view situations more objectively and consider alternative means of dealing with them. Negative thought patterns, on the other hand, correlate with feeling overwhelmed and defeated. As a result, the person tends to accept the situation without seeking other alternatives.

Thus, it is extremely necessary to pay attention to our thoughts when we are being criticized and, most importantly, to make sure they are not negatively affecting the way we perceive criticism from others.

Success and Failure

Building confidence is closely linked to how we define success and interpret failure. What is your definition of success? I've never met anyone who wasn't seeking success, yet when I ask people for their definition of the term, few could tell me what it meant to them.

The best definition of success that I've ever heard came from the sixty-five-year-old wife of a highly successful heart surgeon. She said, "Success is getting what you want, then wanting what you get."

Some interviewees in the study viewed success as a series of accomplishments that leads to the eventual achievement of a desired end result. People who saw success in this way were better able to regard criticism simply as part of the process, rather than an end in itself. They also perceived criticism as "corrective information," which, when accepted and acted on, could lead them closer to the attainment of a particular goal. Similarly, when these interviewees failed to achieve a certain goal, they were able to put it quickly into perspective. Instead of interpreting the failure as evidence of their total worthlessness, they treated it as a temporary inconvenience—and, more important, as an opportunity to learn.

OTHER FACTORS THAT COLOR OUR PERCEPTION OF CRITICISM

So far we've been considering a number of factors that affect our confidence and color the way we perceive criticism. But there are other factors that need to be considered because they affect the criticism process as well. These factors include the level of trust and acceptance that exists between us and the giver, the choice of words and phrases used to communicate the criticism, the style of delivery, and the time and place where criticism is delivered. Let's highlight these elements that color the way we perceive criticism.

The Relationship with the Giver

The identity of the person who gives us information influences whether we perceive the information as criticism or as something else, such as advice, commentary, or an aspect of a power play. Interestingly, interviewees often interpreted such comments from people who played an important role in their life as *advice*, not as criticism. Advice was also used in place of criticism when the outcome was positive. The distinction between advice and criticism is an important one to clarify. If someone gives you advice, he or she is pointing out what you can do about a negative situation, without actually expecting you to take action on it. For instance, say you get home from work and suddenly remember that you've got people coming for dinner. You call your best friend in a panic. He says, "Calm down. You've still got an hour and a half. You can put together a really good chicken salad in that time, or you can do something with fish. Fish doesn't take long to cook." Your friend really has no vested interest in whether you make the chicken salad, the fish, or simply have Chinese food delivered—after all, he's not coming for dinner—so you accept his suggestions as useful advice. Suppose, on the other hand, you call your mother in the same situation and she says, "You're such a scatterbrain; you always leave everything to the last minute." In this case, you are receiving criticism. Your mother hopes you will take action—to become better organized. If you fail to do so, she will continue to criticize you in the future for forgetfulness and procrastination.

Our study respondents reveal that, of all the people we interact with, our boss is one of the few from whom we *don't* mind receiving criticism. Our bosses do pay our salaries but, more importantly, as we mentioned earlier, a Bright Enterprises study indicated that people *expect* honest feedback in the workplace. They look to their bosses as colleagues who will not only offer praise but will also point out weaknesses.

The people from whom survey participants most resented receiving criticism were in-laws, followed by one's mate and one's subordinates at work. Not only is criticism from in-laws most resented, but their criticism is least likely to be acted on. Only 14 percent of the respondents in the Simmons Market Research Bureau/Bright Enterprises study stated that they think it is important to take corrective action on criticism they receive from an in-law, and only 11 percent will actually take action on that criticism.

If a child criticizes a parent, fathers will resent it more than mothers. However, criticism *from* parents will be resented more by women than by men.

Whether we take action on criticism doesn't always correlate with our feelings of resentment. For example, as we've just seen, we resent criticism most from our in-laws and are least likely to change our behavior as a result of their criticism. But while we also resent criticism from our mate, we will probably take action on the criticism he or she has given us.

Because we have a stronger emotional attachment to our mate than to our boss, it's not startling to find out that we tend to personalize criticism more from our mate.

The nature of our job also helps to determine how we react to criticism. According to the Simmons Market Research Bureau/ Bright Enterprises results, people in managerial positions are more likely to change their behavior when being criticized by bosses, subordinates, and co-workers than are people who do not work in a managerial capacity.

Choice of Words and Phrases

Many interviewees said that what bothers them most about criticism is not the act itself or who is giving it, but rather how it is given. Phrases and word choices can easily polarize the giver and the receiver and cause the receiver to arbitrarily reject any information contained in the criticism. Phrases guaranteed to irritate include the following: "You've done a wonderful job on this project, but ...", "This is awful, how could you be so stupid?", "If you really cared about this, you would have ...", "I can't believe you'd make such a dumb mistake." And so on. Some lines that infuriated a group of senior executive women included: "You're like all the other women that work in this office", "You shouldn't have said that; it was the wrong thing to say"; and "If you were a man, this never would have happened."

In addition, certain specific words may bother you and cause you to lose your focus. These words may include: "should have," "must," "have to," "selfish," "aggressive," "stupid," "irresponsible," "bad attitude," "failure," and "disappointment." For some people, a simple "no" at the beginning of a sentence can trigger a negative reaction.

Remember, words can be very powerful sources of emotional arousal. As Dr. Karl Albrecht discusses in his *Brain Power Book*, the brain constructs and stores a number of sensory patterns as a result of repeated experiences; only a few cues are needed to activate these patterns. The advantage of pattern thinking is its efficiency in day-to-day activities. One can quickly draw conclusions based on small bits of information. The disadvantage, especially when one is a receiver of criticism, is that one can easily become a prisoner of his or her thinking patterns and fail to discriminate between what is happening now and what happened in the past.

As a receiver, it's important that you recognize which phrases and word choices serve as triggers for conditioned emotional responses and prevent you from utilizing criticism as new information. Simply being aware of these words and phrases may be enough to help you to avoid overreacting and thereby losing control.

Style of Delivery

In addition to the actual words spoken, such subtleties as inflection, volume, and the rate at which the words are spoken profoundly affect how people perceive what is being said. We are all familiar with Jack Benny's famous "Well . . ." Because of his masterful intonation, Benny was able to capture exasperation, mild surprise, disdain, and a number of other feelings in that single word, to the continual delight of his audience.

The same process occurs when someone is transmitting information via criticism. The inflection placed on a single word can express volumes to the receiver. Consider the phrase "You did a good job, *but* . . ." If the word "but" is given no particular emphasis, it functions simply as a conjunction, connecting the first statement with what follows. It is likely that the receiver will accept the subsequent words as a statement of fact or possibly something akin to advice. However, a pause before the word "but" to add importance, or a change in the volume of the speaker's voice as the word is spoken, turns the following words into an analysis of what is wrong with the "good job." The receiver now thinks that criticism may be intended. He or she becomes alarmed, and the whole process of interpreting criticism that we discussed in chapter 3 must be put into operation.

Similarly, the giver's rate of speech can influence the way in which the receiver perceives the information. Words that are delivered rapidly may be viewed as being perfunctory or unimportant, while deliberate, slow speech can give the impression of being contrived or give the words greater significance than warranted.

Many people will reject criticism if the giver raises his or her voice. One president of a research firm confessed that she will not listen to criticism if the giver insists on shouting. She becomes so upset when someone yells at her that she can't listen. She tells potential critics, "If you want me to hear what you have to say, please don't yell."

Timing and Criticism

The time and place in which criticism is presented are often critical factors in how the receiver will perceive the information. Public criticism, for instance, tends to promote a host of emotional responses in the receiver that makes it extremely difficult for him or her to evaluate the giver's true intent. If the receiver feels strongly that the giver's intention is to embarrass or humiliate more than to help, the receiver could very well reject the criticism and perhaps become outwardly hostile.

Also, the timing of the criticism is an essential factor. Consider a baseball player who has just finished a game in which he delivered four hits, including a home run, and who is being criticized by his manager for committing a fielding error that did not affect the outcome of the game. Because of his high level of self-confidence and his good feelings about his overall performance, the player is likely to be receptive to the manager's criticism. He will consider it to be valuable information that is intended to help improve his already outstanding playing. But if the same player has just finished a game in which he struck out three times and hit into a costly double play, he will be much more likely to feel hurt and embarrassed by similar criticism. His self-confidence will be shaky, and he will tend to be more sensitive to any negative comments about his playing. Unless this player has an unusually good relationship with his manager, including mutuality of high expectations, it will be difficult for him to appreciate the manager's intent or even to accept the criticism at all.

The Giver's Responses

A giver who is overly involved in trying to deliver his or her criticism may fail to respond appropriately to the receiver. In other cases, the giver might be angry with or uninterested in the receiver and also respond inadequately. Unhelpful responses on the part of the giver may take several forms. The giver may fail to listen properly to what the receiver has to say or to allow the receiver to speak at all. Furthermore, the giver may adopt an intimidating demeanor, or he or she may avoid answering direct questions asked by the receiver, or may show a general lack of sensitivity to the position of the receiver in such situations. Whatever form such a response takes, whether intentional or not, if it is inadequate or unacceptable to the receiver, it can destroy any effort to communicate and can cause the receiver to reject the criticism.

Criticism That Hurts

The nature of the criticism itself is an important factor that can have a tremendous impact on us, especially if it hurts. As a receiver of criticism, you should know the types of comments and circumstances that are likely to upset you the most. Having this awareness will better enable you to remain in control and will minimize the chances of your taking the criticism personally. For instance, respondents in the Simmons Market Research Bureau/Bright Enterprises research study were asked to indicate which of eleven types of criticism would hurt them the most.

Review each of the choices and decide which types of criticism would hurt *you* the most:

1. Being criticized for something that was not my responsibility.
2. Being criticized because of my gender.
3. Being criticized for something that I know is true about myself.
4. Being criticized for something that I know is untrue about myself.
5. Being criticized for my knowledge and creativity.
6. Being criticized for something I was doing but was unaware of.
7. Being criticized for the way I manage people.
8. Criticism that questions my integrity.
9. Being criticized for having a poor attitude.
10. Being criticized for my job performance.
11. Being criticized for my appearance.

Compare your responses with those of the respondents in our study. Both men and women, for instance, agreed that having their integrity questioned hurts the most, followed by being criticized for job performance. An important point to keep in mind here is that women are hurt more easily than men and that it's especially important for women to make sure not to personalize criticism to the point that they miss the potential value of the message and destroy the messenger in the process. In the workplace, inability to take criticism well can be devastating to one's career. In the world of sports, coaches emphasize to their athletes the importance of learning to lose gracefully, and the same is true on the job. Employees also need to learn how to accept praise, just as they need to learn to accept criticism.

CRITICISM AND STRESS

Unlike advice, criticism contains the built-in expectation that some kind of action will result from it. There is an implicit or explicit suggestion that the receiver needs to make a change of some kind. Some of us, however, tend to resist change. Underlying this resistance, perhaps, is our inability to predict what will happen. When we are asked to make a change, there is a chance of our becoming more successful; at the same time, we could end up doing worse. We know that if we *don't* make any changes, at least the outcome will be more or less predictable. Some of us opt for predictability in our lives, rather than risk making a change and seizing a possible opportunity to improve.

Being confronted with the fact that someone wants us to change can be a keen source of stress.

Let's talk a bit now about the ways stress can be managed to help each of us stay in better control.

To begin, handling the stress produced from criticism is easier if criticism is kept in proper perspective. As has been mentioned before, even though criticism is negative, it can provide you with an opportunity to grow and improve if you determine that the comments are valid. As the receiver, remember the control lies with you. You have the power to sort out the motives behind the criticism, to evaluate whether the giver is off limits and to decide whether the criticism can be backed up by specifics. You then take control over whether or not you accept the criticism and what is the best course of action to take. Whether or not you personalize the criticism also lies within your control.

Luther, a corporate manager, is a good example of someone who practiced turning criticism around to his advantage. Unbeknownst to Luther and his colleagues, his company's field managers rated all their corporate-level managers. The ratings ranged from A, the highest, to E. Luther discovered, much to his chagrin, that he was given only a C.

His initial reaction was one of shock and disbelief. He had always viewed himself as a top-level performer. The idea of being a C person occupied most of his thoughts, and he became depressed.

Luther isn't exactly sure when or why it happened, but he started to reexamine his thoughts and his C grade. Instead of personalizing the criticism and accepting the evaluation as permanent, Luther began to analyze what lay behind his poor rating. He began to take several facts into account. First, he had been in his position for only seven months, so perhaps he hadn't had enough time to prove himself as an A manager. Second, unlike most of his peers, Luther is rather reserved and he rarely joined his associates for lunch or for drinks after work. He also knew that he sometimes had trouble getting his ideas across to his co-workers. Besides being a very progressive thinker, Luther was well read and when he spoke, he sometimes used obscure words and made reference to various experts with whom his audience was unfamiliar.

Instead of viewing the situation as eternal, Luther began to view it as a challenge. First, he made an effort to expand his lines of communication with his field staff in order to gain a clearer understanding of their expectations and opinions. Whenever possible, he worked harder to be more social. Rather than eating lunch at his desk, Luther began going out with members of his field staff. He also made a conscious attempt to prepare his comments before speaking and screened out words and references that his peers might find esoteric. Luther's next rating was much higher.

As Luther admitted, turning this situation from a disaster to a challenge wasn't easy. The corporate business environment is neither kind nor generous. It takes a certain type of inner strength to keep a person going, and it helps to understand that the receiver of criticism has a great deal of control—if he or she decides to use it.

Looking at the reasons for his C grade may have helped Luther realize that it's difficult to operate from the premise that you have to be superior in everything. As Bob Swain, chairman of Swain & Swain, a New York–based outplacement service, and author of *Out the Organization*, told me, "It's easy for us to get confused and lose our focus. Organizations operate with zero defects and it's almost as if success is equated with perfection. Applying that premise to ourselves creates a lot of stress and turns 'criticism' into a threat. A more realistic underlying premise to work with is to accept the fact that we are not perfect. We don't have to be competent and good at everything."

Building from this foundation changes our focus. It's no longer relevant to concentrate on being perfect because our premise establishes that we aren't perfect in the first place. Instead, we shift our focus toward consistently improving performance. A C rating is no longer an end in itself; it's simply an indication that improvement is possible.

Furthermore, adopting this premise enables us to transform criticism from a negative threat into a positive challenge. Perhaps it's their adherence to this perspective that explains why so many of the people interviewed in our study were empowered by criticism. Even though criticism itself is negative, it can trigger positive insights.

Using this premise also helps us to realize that we cannot reasonably expect to respond well to every piece of criticism we receive. From one day to the next, or from one situation to another, our confidence, mood, and inner strength vary. When our defenses are low, it's easier for criticism to be received emotionally. Our ability to objectively view criticism as information is diminished.

What's needed in these situations are self-adjusting tools that we can implement easily and effectively to help us regain greater control over the situation and ourselves. These tools are called "Quick Charges" because, as a CEO of a telecommunications company told me years ago, these tools are used instantly. They give you the "burst of energy" needed to better handle uncomfortable situations.

Besides being used instantly to handle criticism better and stay in control, people cannot detect when you are using these techniques. Also, their effectiveness does not depend on the reactions of others.

Let's explore some situations in which Quick Charges can be advantageous.

QUICK CHARGES: TECHNIQUES FOR HANDLING CRITICISM ON THE SPOT

Before we explore the usage of various Quick Charges, let's first take a self-effectiveness test. Unlike other tests, this one will not

	1 Almost never effective	2 Rarely effective	3 Sometimes effective	4 Frequently effective	5 Most of the time effective	6 Almost always extremely effective
1. How good are you at staying cool when some-one is criticizing you?						
2. How effectively can you eliminate any knots that form in your stomach when receiving criticism? (If this one doesn't apply to you, you're lucky. Simply move to the next question.)						
3. How well do you listen when someone is crit-icizing you?						
4. How effectively can you organize your thoughts and recall information while being criticized?						
5. How effectively do you handle intimidation from another person while being criticized?						
6. How effectively do you respond as an adult when someone criticizes you as if you were a child?						
7. How effective are you at not personalizing criticism?						
8. How effectively do you let go of criticism?						

give you any final grade, only an awareness of how effectively you deal with various parts of the criticism process.

For each of the following questions, rate yourself on a 1 to 6 scale. A 6 indicates that you are extremely effective in dealing with that particular situation. A 1 means that you feel you have a lot of room for improvement.

Before we go on to consider each of these questions, it might be interesting to point out that most people give themselves only a 3 or 4 rating on these items. Either respondents are highly self-critical (which is probably the case) or have spent very little time in learning to manage themselves in a variety of stress-producing situations.

The quick charges that we'll next look at have been used successfully by thousands of people over the years. In fact, you probably use many of them already. As you read on, much of what you already do will be reinforced. At the same time, some of your skills may be further refined. I hope that these quick charges will provide you with a new insight on how to handle criticism better.

Let's now consider the questions on the self-effectiveness test. We'll discuss each one in turn and will introduce at least one quick charge for managing your stress positively.

1. *How good are you at staying cool when someone is criticizing you?*

Respondents in my workshops and seminars typically give themselves a low rating on this question, and the findings of the Simmons research survey confirmed this response. Our quick charge for keeping your cool is applicable both at work and at home.

When you sense that you are losing your ability to control yourself, stop talking (this in and of itself may have an immediate calming effect) and simultaneously practice the *breathing quick charge*. First inhale slowly through your nose and then exhale through your nose even more smoothly and slowly. At the same time, relax all your muscles, progressing from your head and face all the way down to your toes. Many people describe the sensation of relaxing their muscles as akin to a wave of calm that rolls downward through their body. Others envision a relaxing scene while they are exhaling.

It's valuable to ask yourself two questions during the exhalation phase. First, "What do I want?" This helps you to remember what you are trying to accomplish, something you may have lost sight of during your interaction with the giver. Second, "Have I really been listening to the other person?" Too often we hear only what we want to hear.

You may well be wondering how you can do all this at the same time that someone is criticizing you. You can. The reason you can is because it all occurs at lightning speed. Be assured that it takes a lot more time to explain the actions than to do them.

After you have carefully considered the two questions posed above and start to speak, be sure to talk slowly and calmly. This will help you to control your emotions.

2. *How effectively can you eliminate any knots that form in your stomach?*

Not everyone gets knots in their stomach when under stress. However, for people who do, here is a good way to eliminate those knots—practice the *stomach quick charge.*

    A. Inhale normally and hold your breath.
    B. At the same time, contract your abdominal muscles and hold for approximately three seconds.
    C. Exhale slowly as you imagine that your stomach is being coated with your favorite antacid, and that the contents of your stomach are settling down. This process can be likened to a rough, choppy lake turning into a smooth, placid body of water.

Depending on the severity of your stomach knots, you might want to repeat the exercise two or three more times. One advantage of this quick charge is that you can talk at the same time you're relaxing yourself.

Instead of stomach knots, stress may cause you to tighten your jaw. If this is the case, you can ease the tension by performing the following "jaw massage" quick charge, suggested by Dr. Jonathan

Curzon, a New York–based chiropractor. While the other person is speaking, instead of letting your tension mount, press on both sides of your jawbone just below your earlobe, preferably with your thumbs or middle fingers. Hold for a few seconds. At the same time, imagine that your tensions are being released. Repeating this process several times during a high-stress conversation is valuable. If you don't mind looking like a fish, you can reduce the tension even more quickly by opening and closing your mouth several times while pressing your jawbones. An ideal time to use this technique is when the other person momentarily leaves the room or turns away from you for a few seconds. Be discreet! I am by no means recommending that you make a spectacle of yourself. In fact, you should keep in mind that you can use this quick charge just as effectively after your conversation is finished and you're back at your own desk.

3. How well do you listen when someone is criticizing you?

We tend to listen to what we want to hear, so we may fool ourselves into believing that we are good listeners when in reality we aren't. Being a good listener is probably one skill that everyone can improve upon. That's not a criticism, it's a fact!

A few points to keep in mind when we are listening to someone.

First, there are different styles of listening, just as there are different styles of speaking. How you listen depends on the situation and on your intentions. When you're in a stressful situation, such as receiving criticism, it's important to *listen for understanding.* Listening for understanding is the alternative to listening for agreement. When you listen to understand, you tend to assume the role of a learner. There's a tendency to keep an open mind, while directing your energy toward seeking out information.

This is in contrast to listening for agreement, which changes your orientation toward listening. When you listen for agreement, you focus more on yourself and how you view a particular situation. You tend to judge what the other person is saying in an effort to determine if it is in agreement with what you believe.

The disadvantages to listening for agreement when being criticized are obvious—besides missing the total message, you are more apt to personalize what is being said. The resultant outcome is increased stress.

The thoughts and expectations that we bring to a situation can also affect the way we listen. Researchers continue to remind us that the expectations we have not only affect how we perceive reality but also affect the reality itself.

Furthermore, if we are optimistic, according to Michael F. Scheler, a psychologist at Carnegie-Mellon University, we are better able to handle stress than if we are pessimistic. Scheler's research found that optimists tend to respond to disappointments by formulating a plan of action and asking other people for help and advice. Pessimists, on the other hand, more often react to such setbacks by trying to forget the whole thing or assuming that there is nothing they can do to change the situation.

As we apply these findings to the listening process, it becomes evident that we can gain much by keeping a positive outlook while we are listening. Besides remaining open to what others have to say to us, we are more likely to be attentive because we are seeking to develop an appropriate plan of action.

Remember that listening is a skill, and, as with any skill, you need to practice it regularly. For instance, as soon as you suspect that your mind may be wandering, steer it back toward the conversation and concentrate on what the other person is saying. In addition, avoid doing other tasks, like approving invoices or sorting papers, while someone is speaking to you. Although it is hard to determine how much this will improve your ability to listen, it will certainly help to convey to the other person that you are listening to him or her. To ensure that you're listening, it's helpful to practice the *"rephrase" quick charge.* This is a technique you may already be familiar with: using your own words, you repeat back to the other person what he or she has said. You're not only clarifying the communication, but you're making sure that you both are in agreement before launching further into the conversation.

When you become a good listener, you'll "listen with ears that can hear" observes Barbara Alvord, research director for the western region of the Equitable Financial Companies.

4. *How effectively can you organize your thoughts and recall information while being criticized?*

When you are being criticized, thinking clearly is really a challenge, especially when your stress level is high. Handling this situation effectively centers around playing for more time in order to help you regain control. The quick charges to use in this situation are best referred to as *time builders.* One effective time builder is simply to ask the other person to repeat the last thing that he or she said. While he or she is doing this, you can organize your mind. The actual time needed to gather your thoughts is minimal; as communications experts remind us, we think at about 500 to 600 words per minute, while we speak at about 125 to 150 words per minute. So as the other person repeats his statement, you have ample time to assemble your thoughts.

An even better, but more sophisticated, time builder is to repeat what you think the person said, or asked, but in rephrasing it deliberately repeat one point *incorrectly.* The benefits of this time builder are striking. Not only do you give yourself the time that you need to regain control, but the other person, if he or she is listening, quickly detects your error and, in the process of correcting what you said, will inevitably add some additional thoughts. This extra information may be just what you need to sort out the intention behind the criticism.

When using this quick charge you'll want to be very careful at what "error" you elect to use. Because of the impact of this quick charge, it's advisable to use it sparingly in any one conversation.

Other ways to stall for time include lighting up a cigarette or, for an even longer break, a pipe. If you don't smoke, or if smoking is not allowed at your place of business, you can always drop something or say that you don't understand or didn't hear what was being said. You may even excuse yourself for a minute to go to the restroom. These are all socially acceptable quick charges for gaining the additional time you need to reestablish control of the situation.

5. *How effectively do you handle intimidation from another person while being criticized?*

Sometimes we can predict whether a certain person is likely to intimidate us; at other times, intimidation takes us by surprise. Here are two quick charges that will help minimize intimidation from anyone, whether at work or at home.

The first *intimidation quick charge* comes from our understanding of nonverbal communication. You probably are aware of the fact that the eyes are considered the most powerful tools for nonverbal communication. After all, our language is full of sayings such as "If looks could kill . . . ," "The eyes are the windows of the soul," or "She stares right through you." Etiquette teaches us to look at someone when he or she is talking to us to encourage trust. Conversely, to look away is considered a sign of distrust. A polite way to eliminate feelings of intimidation that come with the way a person looks at us is to look directly at the person as he or she speaks, but focus your attention between the speaker's eyes at the bridge of his or her nose. This action has two results: first, the person's gaze doesn't penetrate through you (it's as if you have constructed an imaginary wall to protect you from the intense look of the other person) and, second, you'll be able to think more clearly and regain your focus.

Our second intimidation quick charge is simply to say, "Excuse me?" in a firm but questioning tone of voice. This works extremely well when the giver is getting carried away with his or her criticism. When you say, "Excuse me?," the other person is being asked to repeat all the outlandish charges that he or she has just made.

Keep in mind that both of these quick charges are skills like the other ones we have introduced—they need to be practiced.

6. *How effectively do you respond as an adult when someone criticizes you as if you were a child?*

"You gave a terrible presentation this morning! How could you embarrass our department in front of the CEO like that?" Does something about this rebuke sound vaguely familiar? If it does, there's a good reason why: your parents probably scolded you in much the same way when you were a child.

Many givers of criticism unfortunately dole out their comments as if they were talking to a six-year-old. While this may not be the best way for them to deliver the criticism (we will discuss this point further in chapters 6 and 8), what we're concerned about here is how you respond.

Experts in the field of transactional analysis like Eric Berne and Thomas Harris have come up with two effective *adulthood quick charges* to deal with a giver who comes across as an irate parent. Using the first technique, you agree with what the giver has said; in fact, you *elaborate* on it. If your boss tells you that you gave a terrible presentation, reply, "You're right. I feel so ashamed. I can't believe what an appalling presentation it was." In all probability, the giver will then say, somewhat reassuringly, "Well, it wasn't all *that* bad."

Agreeing with the criticism in this manner is an effective way to avoid having to defend yourself in a potentially volatile confrontation. Instead, you encourage the giver to back down from his or her initial anger and discuss the issue more rationally.

The second quick charge you can try in these cases is to reject being treated like a child by responding like an adult. If your boss berates you for your "terrible" presentation, calmly ask him or her, "What specifically was so awful? I'd really appreciate it if you'd let me know." This type of approach reminds the giver that he or she is dealing with an adult and should be treating you as such. It frees you from having to defend yourself in the heat of the moment; instead, you are asking grown-up questions to clarify the negative information you are receiving about your performance. And, as we've seen repeatedly, the clearer the information you receive as criticism, the better able you will be to evaluate its worth and act on it appropriately.

7. *How effective are you at not personalizing criticism?*
If you are a woman and feel uncomfortable about giving yourself a low rating on this question, don't. Our research showed that

in *every* relationship surveyed, women personalize criticism to a much greater degree than men. It doesn't matter whether the criticism comes from mother, father, friend, sibling, boss, co-worker, in-law, or children—women tend to take it personally.

Putting sex aside, probably the main consideration when responding to this question is that it depends on who is criticizing and the nature of the criticism.

As it relates to married couples, the criticism study showed that partners make a concerted effort to identify the true motives behind their spouse's criticism. If one spouse criticizes the other, the receiver will try to determine whether the criticism is deserved or whether the giver has just had a rough day and is relieving stress. However, in the latter case, the receiver, whether male or female, will be strongly inclined to personalize the criticism.

When we refer to "personalizing" criticism what do we really mean? Are we saying that when someone criticizes us it hurts and we become upset? If this is what personalizing criticism means, then perhaps it's okay, because that could be exactly what the giver is intending to do. Some of us need to hurt before we will take any action.

On the other hand, if personalizing criticism means that while the criticism is being communicated we can't listen or think properly, then perhaps what we are saying is that instead of personalizing the criticism, we are "emotionalizing" it. If this is the case then one way to minimize "emotionalizing" criticism is to practice the *depersonalizer quick charge*. Take something that you wear regularly—a favorite piece of jewelry or an article of clothing, such as a tie or belt—and mentally imagine it as a filtering device with a built-in rechargeable battery. This filtering device runs at all times. Its function is to screen information you receive from others.

Your built-in filtering device analyzes carefully what others are saying. As an example, if a client to whom you have just given a presentation tells you, "You did a marvelous job," the filtering device is activated. Before you accept the praise, you quickly examine your performance in relationship to your client's comment. If your evaluation agrees with the client's remark, you accept the praise. If it doesn't, you may accept only part of the praise or reject it altogether. Regardless of your filtering system's conclusion, you politely thank your client for taking the time to comment favorably on your presentation.

The filtering mechanism operates in the same way when the comment is critical. Before you accept or act on criticism, your filtering system is asking questions such as "Who is this person? What is the purpose behind this criticism? Where is the giver coming from? Can this criticism be backed up? What can I learn from it?"

Your imaginary filter helps you to minimize your tendency to personalize the criticism and to view what is being said as simply information. In addition, it helps you to focus on what can be learned instead of only the negative aspects of the situation. This filtering system also ought to enable you to take appropriate action and recognize its relationship to your goals.

There is a learning phase associated with this quick charge. It could take about one week to see some improvement, and with criticism from people to whom you are very close, it may take longer. Once you've mastered this quick charge, don't be disappointed if you slip up every now and then. Remember, you aren't perfect! It happens to everyone. To expedite your recovery, however, you might try one of the following *"big picture" quick charges.*

These quick charges help us to avoid making too much of an unimportant situation. Practice them by reminding yourself of any or all of the following statements:

"Only doctors, nurses, and law enforcement officers deal with life-and-death issues. I've simply been criticized. Is it a life-or-death issue?"

"Five years from now, how important will this situation be?"

"And this, too, shall pass."

Repeating these truisms to yourself helps to keep the criticism in perspective. It shifts the focus from the momentary horror of the criticism to the bigger picture—the content of the criticism, and the action that you can take.

8. *How effectively do you let go of criticism?*

Holding on to criticism for days on end isn't very healthy, nor does it do much for one's optimistic outlook. Brooding over criticism *is* a means of acting on it, but is this action what you really want to be doing?

Building from our premises that we aren't perfect and that criticism is designed to bring about action that will lead us closer to a desired end result will then make it easier to use the following *paperbasket quick charge.*

This skill is practiced by mentally writing down all your thoughts, especially your troublesome ones, on an imaginary piece of paper. After mentally placing all your thoughts on the paper, visualize crumpling up the paper and throwing it into the wastepaper basket, where it immediately gets burned. As with some of the other quick charges we've discussed, depending upon the severity of the situation, it may be necessary to practice this skill several times. Remember, after you've carefully examined and learned from your mistake, it's important to "let go" of criticism.

Chapter 5

CRITICISM CLOSE UP: GIVING IT

Mary Jo, the managing editor of a business magazine, is sitting at her desk staring nervously at her watch. In five minutes, Peter, an editorial assistant, is due to show up for his performance review, and Mary Jo has several bones to pick with him. Peter is popular with his co-workers and his editing skills are excellent. However, he is supposed to be at work at 9:00 A.M. to take calls from the magazine's European correspondents, and he is often late. Secondly, his desk is always a mess. The other day, one of the senior editors was searching through the piles on Peter's desk for something he'd put there earlier and instead found—to his utter dismay—a minor assignment he'd given Peter a week or two before that was sitting untouched at the bottom of a stack of papers. Mary Jo thinks that Peter has the potential to be a first-rate editor, but he has to improve his work habits. While she's waiting, she's wondering how best to approach the subject. She's even debating whether it might just be easier to tell him he's doing fine—after all, he's always in by 9:15 or 9:30, and the editing task he forgot to do wasn't a crucial one.

Mary Jo's dilemma is all too common. She, like a great many people, find it more difficult to *give* criticism than to *receive* it! This trait, which may seem surprising and unexpected at first, can be attributed to the fact that most of us prefer to avoid unpleasant confrontations. By simply telling Peter that he's doing a great job, she knows that their meeting will be short and friendly; but he'll continue to miss the calls from London and Paris and will let the work pile up on his desk. If, on the other hand, she takes him to task for his shortcomings, she runs the risk of Peter's objecting to her criticism and embroiling her in a long, heated discussion.

What should Mary Jo do? To answer this question thoroughly, we should first examine *why* people criticize others. We know by now that criticism is an inevitable part of the human experience, but what purpose does it serve?

WHY DO PEOPLE CRITICIZE OTHERS?

There are probably as many specific reasons or motivations for criticism as there are human interactions, but, broadly speaking, as it relates to criticism of others we can divide the reasons into two major categories: positive (productive) and negative (destructive). Negative reasons may include the need to destroy, demoralize, or subjugate the receiver or to vent one's anger or frustration on the receiver in order to feel better themselves. Or the giver may want to impress or placate a third party. Positive reasons for criticism, on the other hand, have only one real purpose: to direct the receiver's behavior in order to lead to a desired end result, like enhanced performance. Mary Jo's planned criticism of Peter could help him to become a better employee, so her reason appears to be positive.

Before you criticize someone, it is important that you be clear about your *motives*. If your motives are positive, fine. But if they are negative, stop yourself! Criticism that is destructively motivated can be devastating and destroy the receiver's self-confidence. Thoughtless or cruel criticism has shattered many people permanently.

So remember: Before you criticize someone, be sure to think

about why you're doing so. If you honestly think that your criticism will help the receiver in some way achieve a desired end result, then you're on the right track.

THE PREMISES BEHIND CRITICISM

Whether or not the giver is aware of it, criticism generally is based on one or more of the following premises or assumptions:

1. The giver is right and the receiver is wrong. For example, Mary Jo assumes that Peter is wrong to come in late and leave work undone, and that she is right to criticize him for it.

2. The giver disapproves of the receiver's behavior. This is related to the above premise, but it is important to note that the degree of disapproval is unknown to the receiver until the giver voices it. For instance, if Mary Jo tells Peter, "Basically, you're doing a great job, but you really should be here at nine," the degree of implied disapproval is less than if she says, "You're not getting in on time, and it's seriously impairing your job performance." Also, in the business environment, givers of criticism are often placed in the position of having to deliver criticism based on management policy—even when they don't agree with that policy. For example, Mary Jo may not care personally that Peter has missed a couple of calls or forgotten to edit a minor assignment, but ultimately she is responsible for the performance of those under her. If she fails to ask him to correct his behavior, she herself may have to take the heat from her superiors.

3. The giver assumes that the receiver will somehow alter his or her behavior as a result of the criticism. For instance, Mary Jo assumes that if she criticizes Peter for his lateness, he will probably make an effort to get to work on time if he wants to keep his job. Similarly, a mother who chides her daughter for not cleaning her room will expect that her daughter will try to be a little tidier. To ensure that the expectation is conveyed, the criticism must be worded in such a way that will make the receiver realize that the

criticism is important and that taking action is expected. The difficulty here is obvious; when action is not taken or action is inappropriate, it frequently results in disappointment and the need for further criticism.

THE RECEIVER IS IN CONTROL

A mythical premise on which criticism is often based is that the giver is in control when he or she criticizes the receiver. As we disclosed in chapters 3 and 4, actually, the *receiver* has greater control over the situation. In fact, the control at the onset does lie with the giver, but once the criticism is communicated, the control shifts to the receiver.

How can this be? you may still wonder. Let's take another look at Peter and Mary Jo. If Peter fails to act on Mary Jo's criticism, she may fire him. While this is true, of course, the reality of the situation is far more complex. Once Mary Jo has criticized Peter's performance, the following will occur:

1. Peter will assume control of whether to approve the criticism. He may, for instance, reject the criticism about the assignment he hasn't done because he was told to do it "whenever you have time."

2. Peter will assume control over whether or not to take action. His decision will be based largely on whether the energy required to alter his behavior will yield worthwhile results.

3. Peter will take control over whether to reject the criticism because he may not find Mary Jo a credible critic—she takes two-hour lunches and often leaves the office at 3:30—or because he may not think she has his best interests in mind. He can also reject a criticism whose content is not specific. If Mary Jo says, "There was something you forgot to edit," he may decide the criticism is too vague and he doesn't remember exactly which assignment she's talking about anyway. A nonspecific criticism is difficult to swallow and accept as valid. If the giver cannot provide specifics, then it's best to delay the criticism until enough information is available to make it stick. To help you keep track

of specifics, you might want to start a confidential folder in which you list incidents that support your criticism.

The point to keep in mind here is that as long as the receiver has a choice—whether to accept the criticism or not, whether to take action or not—he or she is in control.

THE PREPARATION PHASE: INCREASING THE GIVER'S CONTROL

Where does this leave the giver? How can the giver increase his or her degree of control? We've seen that once the criticism has been expressed, control shifts to the receiver. So it is *before* the criticism is delivered that the giver has the most control. The preparation phase, that period prior to delivery of the criticism, is the optimum period of the giver's control.

If the giver hasn't carefully thought about the reasons for offering the criticism, and the way it should be delivered, the criticism may backfire.

The following case history is illustrative: Dave services automatic tellers for a midwestern bank. The job involves frequent visits to the branch offices. Dave's boss has called him in for a review and criticized several aspects of his performance at the branches. Dave retorted, "How do you know? You haven't once been out to the branches yourself!" Dave rejected his boss's criticism because he felt it lacked credibility and validity. Clearly, this was not the reaction that Dave's boss either wanted or expected; his attempt at criticism definitely was not successful.

To increase the likelihood that your criticism will be successful—that is, that it will bring about the desired changes in the receiver's performance—the giver should focus carefully on the preparation phase. Careful preparation to give criticism has the following advantages:

- The giver has a chance to think about the effects on the big picture and what is to be achieved.
- The giver can reflect on the content of the criticism, its credibility as perceived by the receiver, and the way in which

the criticism should be presented in the framework of the situation. Carefully prepared criticism has the greatest chance of being accepted by the receiver. By planning in advance how and what to say, the giver will run less of a risk of offending or alienating the receiver and be more likely to affect the receiver's behavior in a constructive way.

THE GIVER'S FLOWCHART

As you prepare to deliver criticism, refer to the flowchart on page 83. If you take yourself through each of the steps outlined on the flowchart, you will maximize the chances that your criticism will be received. The flowchart cannot, of course, guarantee that your criticism will be successful or lead to positive action, but it will help you to ensure the quality of your criticism's content, delivery, and credibility.

Step I. Evaluate and Focus

Consider the action you want the receiver to take. If you find that you cannot identify a specific action, then you should probably not deliver the criticism. In our study, interviewees frequently reported that the toughest form of criticism to receive was criticism about which they could take no action. For example, criticizing someone's gender or height can have no productive consequences because the person is powerless to change these factors. At worst, such criticism will frustrate and even antagonize the receiver. At best, the receiver will simply ignore it.

If the giver believes that the receiver will be able to take action, the following two questions need to be addressed:

1. Is the receiver capable of behaving appropriately?
2. Is there enough information upon which to act?

It's important that the receiver not only understands what the desired behavior is but that all the information and resources needed are available to carry out the act successfully. As the giver, if you have any doubts about either of these two points, it's best to

THE GIVER'S FLOWCHART

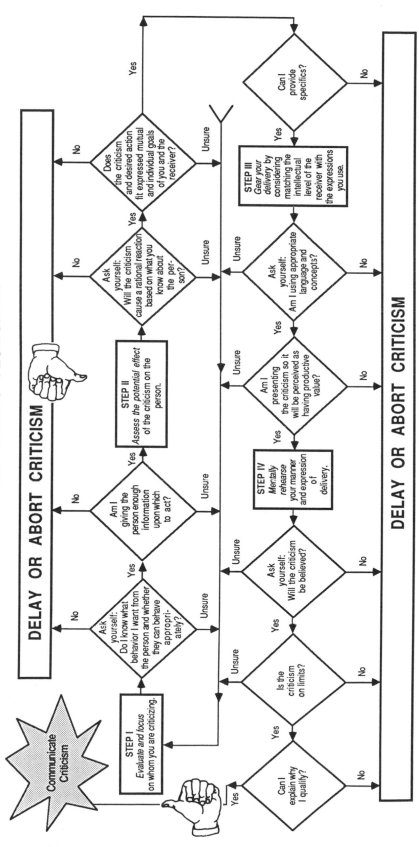

DELAY OR ABORT CRITICISM

DELAY OR ABORT CRITICISM

Communicate Criticism

STEP I *Evaluate and focus* on whom you are criticizing.

Ask yourself: Do I know what behavior I want from the person and whether they can behave appropriately?

Am I giving the person enough information upon which to act?

STEP II *Assess the potential effect* of the criticism on the person.

Ask yourself: Will the criticism cause a rational reaction based on what you know about the person?

Does the criticism and desired action fit expressed mutual and individual goals of you and the receiver?

STEP III *Gear your delivery* by considering matching the intellectual level of the receiver with the expressions you use.

Can I provide specifics?

Am I using appropriate language and concepts?

Am I presenting the criticism so it will be perceived as having productive value?

STEP IV *Mentally rehearse* your manner and expression of delivery.

Ask yourself: Will the criticism be believed?

Is the criticism on limits?

Can I explain why I qualify?

postpone delivering the criticism. Otherwise, you'll only perpetuate ongoing criticism.

Step II: Assess the Potential Effect

Once you've established that the prospective receiver is capable and informed enough to act—and, indeed, that action is possible—you must next assess if the criticism will potentially cause an irrational reaction. Think about your previous interactions with the receiver. How has he or she reacted to criticism from you in the past? One interviewee, for instance, succinctly stated, "I work very hard at what I do, and I take great pride in my work. As a result, I don't take criticism very well. I don't like being told I've done something wrong."

For best results, it's not necessarily a good practice to criticize someone in the way you would like to be criticized yourself, but rather in the way your *receiver* prefers to be criticized.

In my workshops, I've found that, typically, a majority of the participants say that they prefer criticism to be direct and to the point. A smaller number favor a softer, more indirect approach. If you've made an effort to know the receiver and tried to gauge the style of criticism preferred by him or her, your comments will more likely produce the alterations in performance that you're after.

If, on the other hand, the giver criticizes the receiver simply according to his or her own beliefs about how people should be criticized, the results are likely to be unproductive.

Consider Tom and Linda, two intelligent, career-oriented people who have been married for four years. When Tom criticizes Linda, he says such things as "You'll never be able to pull this one off," "You're not prepared," or "You don't know what you're doing." Linda hates these statements. She regards them as personal attacks that undermine her confidence. Tom, on the other hand, persists in his approach. "Would you rather that I not tell you the truth," he asks her, "when what you're saying or doing is horrible? You have to face reality and stand tough; otherwise, you'll never learn or grow."

Instead of listening and questioning Tom about what she might do better, Linda rejects what he says. It's unfortunate that Tom's attempt to use criticism to change behavior backfires. Instead of getting Linda fired up to take positive action, the outcome is hurt feelings, less confidence, and no action toward improving a situation.

In order to determine how the receiver prefers to be criticized, it's best to just ask. It's guaranteed that you will gain some valuable insights about what adults like or dislike. If you don't know or are unsure about how the person prefers to be criticized, delay the criticism.

You've considered whether the receiver is capable of taking action, and what the person's preferred style of being criticized is. Now it's important to think about whether the criticism and the desired action fit expressed individual and mutual goals and expectations. For instance, if a goal or expectation has not been communicated to the receiver, failing to achieve it cannot be justifiably criticized. In the workplace, this typically occurs among new employees.

Let's look at the example of Jacob and Karen. Suppose Jacob has written a memo to the art department without sending a copy to Karen. She may tell him, "You may not have known this, but I need to see copies of everyone's memos to the art department so that I can keep track of what's going on." In this way, she avoids having to criticize Jacob pointlessly by simply explaining office procedures to him. If she were to tell Jacob brusquely, "You didn't give me a copy of the memo that you sent to the art department," he would probably respond, "No one ever told me I was supposed to," thereby deflecting the criticism back at Karen. The first approach is preferable because Karen clearly defines what's expected—and if the goal is to get copies of memos to her, she accomplishes this without having to take a "blaming" approach, thereby causing Jacob to defend himself.

If you're unsure about whether your goal or expectation has

been communicated to the receiver, you should defer criticizing
and instead inform him or her clearly about what the goal is and
what is expected. If both the giver and receiver know that they
are working toward a mutual objective or goal, it's more likely
that the receiver will take action on criticism when the giver de-
livers it.

For example, you will find that coaches are rarely hesitant to
criticize their athletes and the athletes seldom resent their
coach's comments. Why is this true? The answer most likely lies
in the fact that all are working toward mutually shared goals. If
you can relate criticism to agreed-on goals and objectives, it's
more likely to have the desired effect. People tend to devote time
or energy only to a task that they can associate with some positive end result. At the same time, the receiver's tolerance of the
criticism is likely to increase, as is his or her chance of acting on
the criticism and improving performance.

Furthermore, criticism that is delivered in an atmosphere in
which mutual expectations and acceptance exist helps to build
closer, more trusting relationships, whether between husband
and wife, parent and child, or boss and subordinates. As one
manager told me, "I knew how Ellen preferred to be criticized,
and I practiced it. She recognized this and even though I was
discussing an uncomfortable topic, there was a comfortable feeling about our talk that conveyed to her that I cared about her."
This point can't be emphasized enough.

Acceptance of the criticism is highly dependent upon whether
you answer the question "Can you provide specifics?" In an effort
to ensure that the criticism is perceived as constructive, it's
essential that the giver has specific examples to support the
criticism. If not, the giver runs the risk of being put on the
defensive and having the criticism rejected. Wait until specific
examples are available before delivering the criticism. How long
should you wait? Many of us know that it is best to communicate
criticism as close to the event as possible. There's nothing worse
than to have someone criticize you long after the situation has
occurred. But is it necessary to wait for the person to repeat the

desired behavior several times before saying something? Interviewees from the study had their own preferences, but there appears to be a trend toward immediately telling people what they are doing right and what they are doing wrong.

It's important to keep in mind that people place a high value on receiving honest feedback. In the work environment, people genuinely want their supervisors to let them know how they are performing.

Getting no feedback is devastating because you don't know where you stand. Receiving only positive feedback can create big egos, and they are sometimes difficult to deal with. At the same time, praise that is repeatedly delivered tends to loose its luster and credibility. And constant criticism, with *no* positive feedback, can be devastating. Try to develop a balance.

Step III: Gear Your Delivery

The giver must also take into account the receiver's level of experience and education, making sure not to talk up or down to the individual. When your choice of language, as well as concepts, is geared toward the particular receiver, you are helping to ensure that other motives do not color your criticism and counteract your true purpose. Not only should you tailor your language to suit your receiver, but you may also wish to use visual, auditory, or other sensory aids if the receiver learns best from such devices.

For example, several years ago I was asked to observe the University of Michigan's basketball team because they were having some problems with a few freshman players. The coach requested that I attend a workout session to watch these key players in action. One player, Rob, was always being criticized for fouling up the drills. The head coach felt that he was obstinate and a wise guy, and was even considering dropping him from the team. As I watched Rob go through the elaborate drills that the head coach was explaining verbally to the team, I asked the assistant coach, "Where did Rob come from?"

The assistant coach told me that Rob was a freshman who had come from a low-income area in southern Florida, where he had been raised by an aunt. It struck me that, given Rob's background, perhaps it was inaccurate to describe his attitude as uncooperative. In all likelihood, Rob had grown up playing basketball in the streets, not in a well-equipped gym, and had probably never had a coach watching his every move and telling him what to do next. He had most likely learned to play by watching and then imitating the best players in his neighborhood. Therefore, the coach's rapid verbal instructions might have been difficult for him to grasp.

After the workout, I mentioned my theory to the two coaches. They decided to modify the way they presented the drills to see what would happen. At the next practice session, the head coach first diagrammed the drills on a flip chart and supplemented this visualization with a verbal explanation. Then he asked Rob and a few other players to demonstrate the drill. The new procedure worked. Rob easily learned the drills and became more cooperative as well.

A related approach that can help make criticism more palatable is to talk in terms of concepts that you know the receiver values. As a case in point, consider Adam, one of Bill's managers. Bill has the uncomfortable task of telling Adam that he is being demoted to an area that is less active and pressured. From past experience, Bill knows that Adam doesn't react well to criticism, and he is concerned about how he should present this news to Adam without angering him. Bill considers Adam's goal of being an "ace manager" and recalls that Adam is a great believer in good basics—a concept that Adam has tried to apply on the job. Bill decides to bring up the idea of good basics to help explain the move to the less volatile area. He shows Adam how it will enable him to get a firmer grasp on the basics of good management. Adam, while not totally pleased by the move, does respond more calmly than he has previously and even admits that having more time to spend on managing and less on dealing with crisis situations might help him become a better manager.

Step IV: Mentally Rehearse

No matter how well you plan to deliver your criticism, planning alone isn't enough. You must *mentally rehearse* the experience and must do so as many times as you need to before you feel fully comfortable with what you have to say. Otherwise, you run the risk of having the criticism perceived as unbelievable. Mental rehearsal, like the other steps in the preparation phase, cannot guarantee that your criticism will be effective, but it will work to improve its chances of creating positive results.

There's nothing new about mental rehearsal. Even the Bible reminds us: "As a man thinketh he becometh." But, in recent years, many of us have become increasingly exposed to this concept through the earlier work of Maxwell Maltz, whose ideas are described in his famous book *Psycho-cybernetics*, and with other writers, including Charles A. Garfield, author of *Peak Performance*, and Dr. Gary Wiren and Dr. Richard Coop in their book *The New Golf Mind*.

Mental rehearsal, as we know it today, builds on the wealth of research that has shown that acting out a situation in advance boosts our confidence and effectiveness when we are confronted with the actual situation. Not only does mental rehearsal furnish us with a valuable opportunity to practice giving criticism, but it also helps us to identify any key points we might have left out, like making sure that our gestures and word choices are the most appropriate and that any possible inconsistencies that may convey "mixed messages" are considered and dealt with.

In order to increase your credibility even more—and make the receiver more comfortable with the criticism—you should rehearse a coaching tone, rather than a policing tone. If you speak to the receiver as a trainer, rather than a harsh disciplinarian, you will be far more likely to convey the idea that you have the person's best interests at heart.

Most importantly, mental preparation provides us with an opportunity to become aware of whether we are entering into the situation with prejudicial ideas. If the giver falls into the trap of holding on to prejudicial notions, the giver may help to generate a harmful self-fulfilling prophecy. If, for instance, Mary Jo privately believes that Peter will continue to come in late and she somehow communicates this expectation to him, chances are he will make little effort to be more punctual. For the receiver, it's more difficult to become motivated and perform well when he or she feels that no matter what is done, it still won't be good enough.

As interviewee assistant navy secretary Chase Untermeyer said, "Some people may be worthless—but that should be a final conclusion, not a preliminary one."

Preparing ourselves mentally can immeasurably boost our confidence. If we walk into a potentially difficult meeting having prepared ourselves mentally, we are far more likely to come across as more focused and less defensive. In addition, we will probably be better able to remain calm and to listen intently and constructively. With that heightened air of assurance that mental preparation gives you, the perceiver will be more likely to see you as a believable criticizer.

Step V: Set Limits

One of the last questions the giver needs to ask as a sequential part of the preparation stage is "Is the criticism within limits?" Why, you ask, wouldn't it make more sense to focus on this point earlier in the preparation stage? It's strategic to ask this question now because it is one of the first questions that will cross the receiver's mind. If a receiver views criticism as off limits, he or she will feel completely justified in disregarding it. And whether criticism is within limits or not is a variable that can change very suddenly.

Take, for example, your mate. No matter how much you know and love your spouse, you can be off limits. You would not want to criticize your partner just as he or she is returning home after a particularly awful day at work.

It's tough to know precisely when the giver is off limits. It's best, whenever possible, to check out what's been happening before delivering the criticism.

Take, for example, the person who used to be prompt at returning your phone calls, but suddenly isn't. Instead of chiding the person right away for not returning your calls and risk being perceived as off limits, it might be smarter to begin the conversation by asking, "Gee, this isn't like you. How come you haven't returned my calls?" What if the calls hadn't been returned because he or she had been in the hospital!

Criticism may be off limits not only with respect to timing but to content as well. An obvious example is the in-law who criticizes her daughter-in-law for the way she disciplines her child. When criticism is off limits with respect to content, the receiver quickly determines that the person has *no right* to criticize, as with the example of the mother-in-law.

While you mentally rehearse the delivery of criticism, you'll also want to consider if you can explain why you are qualified to give that criticism. Why consider this issue now? The reason is simple. It is likely to be the first question that will race across the receiver's mind. Like criticism that the receiver regards as off limits, criticism that is communicated from someone who the receiver believes is not qualified will also be rejected quickly. The giver's qualifications are uppermost in the receiver's mind when criticism is taking place.

For example, consider two brothers—Matthew, an aspiring writer who works for a book publisher, and Richard, an aspiring painter who has a sales job at a department store. Matthew shows Richard a story he's written and Richard's only comment is: "I think you may have possibly used too much description." Matthew turns on Richard, saying, "Who are you to be so critical? I majored in English and I read on the job all day. Words are my life. You haven't read a book in years!" I'm sure this is a familiar scene—especially among loved ones.

In loving relationships, individuals are not automatically qualified to deliver criticism. However, many times comments are made about a particular issue in an effort to be supportive. The problem arises, as with Matthew and Richard, when the receiver confuses advice with criticism and personalizes it.

As interviewees in the study explained, the giver's qualifications are equated with having a track record, preferably a successful one, in the area under consideration. What this implies is that authority figures, who have the *right* to criticize, are not automatically qualified to give criticism. A level of trust is needed. Remember, too, as with criticism that is off limits, the receiver has control to reject criticism from someone he or she believes is not qualified.

WHEN NOT TO GIVE CRITICISM

We have covered the basics of preparing to give criticism. Being properly prepared is of utmost importance. Following each of the steps in the flowchart helps to ensure that you are obtaining the information needed to deliver criticism in a way that will be accepted and acted upon by the receiver. If you are unable to answer any of the questions raised in each of the steps, it's advisable either to postpone or abort delivering the criticism. Perhaps we should conclude with a brief checklist of the times when you should *avoid* giving criticism. Criticizing a person under any of the following circumstances will invariably have adverse results:

- When the receiver cannot take any action on the criticism.
- When your motives for criticism are selfish.
- When you are overstressed, angry, impatient, or irritable.
- When you cannot or don't want to mold your criticism to the person's preferred style of receiving it.
- When the receiver will think you are being excessively critical.
- When, based on past experience, you know that the receiver will resent the criticism and take no action on it.
- When the timing is bad—for example, when the person has just suffered a traumatic experience.
- When the criticism is general and you can't back it up adequately.

And, if any of the following conditions apply, you should consider *delaying* the criticism until you are better prepared:

- When you're not sure about how to deliver the criticism so that the person will see it as helpful.
- When you don't know how the person prefers to be criticized.
- When you have not mentally rehearsed your delivery.
- When you're not certain that you will be perceived as a credible or qualified source of criticism.
- When individual and mutual goals and objectives and expectations have not been clearly identified and communicated.

Now that we have taken you through the preparatory steps for giving criticism, let us now move on to discuss specific strategies for ensuring the effective delivery of criticism.

Chapter 6

DELIVERING CRITICISM FOR POSITIVE RESULTS

No matter what the size or function of any organization, it is the responsibility of managers and supervisors to evaluate the performance of others—not only to enhance an employee's personal development but also to ensure that tasks or projects are completed according to specifications, on time and within budget.

The criticism study showed that these fundamental managerial responsibilities are precisely what employees expect of managers. Additionally, employees expect "honest feedback" from managers and they sincerely want those aspects of their performance considered less than acceptable to be brought to their attention.

This finding may startle a manager who has just given a performance review to a subordinate and praised her on nine out of ten points, only to find himself arguing for the next forty-five minutes about his one negative comment. However, as we saw in chapter 5, the way in which criticism is presented can affect significantly how it is received; managers should therefore be well prepared before they deliver criticism. Not until you feel confident that you are properly prepared should you enter into the next phase, which is identified as the "exchange phase." Unlike

94

the "preparation phase," which the giver addresses alone, the exchange phase involves the interaction of both the giver and receiver.

In addition to exploring what we already know about giving criticism, we will target our discussion on ways to overcome some of the common problems linked to giving criticism. The chapter will then discuss the follow-up phase in the criticism process.

We will investigate how to ensure that the criticism exchange ends on a positive note, and then move to the explanation of indirect approaches that can be used to enhance performance and get desired end results from others *without criticizing* them.

The chapter will close with a discussion of the congruency model, designed to establish a proper foundation from which criticism can be launched effectively.

THE EXCHANGE PHASE

Preparing for the criticism process is essential, but it is not enough. We must, of course, also be able to handle ourselves during the exchange phase, when we actually communicate the criticism to the receiver.

This is the phase that most of us are familiar with. In the course of our professional and personal development, each of us has accumulated numerous bits of information on how to effectively deliver criticism. Let's explore how familiar you are with what you should know about delivering criticism.

For each of the statements listed below, indicate whether or not you know about the following guidelines when delivering criticism.

Do you know that you should: Yes   No

1. Accentuate the positive aspects of the person's worth.   ____   ____
2. Listen carefully to others' responses and feelings.   ____   ____
3. Stay calm and unemotional when criticizing.   ____   ____

	Yes	No
4. Use "you," not "we," as in: "You need to improve."	___	___
5. Be specific.	___	___
6. Offer a solution or resolution to the problem.	___	___
7. Be nonjudgmental: "It is my observation."	___	___
8. Be supportive and give good strokes.	___	___
9. Present the criticism in a way that the person can learn from it.	___	___
10. Emphasize how the criticism will help improve his or her performance; give some specific examples.	___	___
11. Be sure not to personally attack the individual or group.	___	___
12. Begin and end on a positive note.	___	___
13. Let the person know it's okay to make a mistake— provided something is learned from it.	___	___
14. Criticize the behavior or task, not the individual.	___	___

If you answered yes to most of these statements, then you closely match what participants in the criticism study said they know about giving criticism.

Problems During the Interactive Stage

No matter how well versed you are in the basics of giving criticism, you may still run into problems when you actually deliver it. In my study, respondents were asked what aspects of giving criticism troubled them the most. The six most common difficulties are:

1. Actually doing it. It's so unpleasant.
2. Picking the right time.
3. Getting started.
4. Handling the exchange.
5. Couching criticism so it's helpful.
6. Keeping criticism from becoming personal.

Let's examine each of these issues:

Actually Doing It—It's So Unpleasant

Giving criticism is rarely pleasant—so don't let that slow you down. There are a number of things that we do in life that are not pleasant, like paying bills or taking tests, but they are necessary.

Instead of focusing on the unpleasantness, direct your energy on viewing criticism in its proper light. As we said earlier, if you think of criticism as a tool to modify the behavior of the receiver and to achieve a mutual goal, rather than seeing it as a personal attack against another person, it will become more palatable and easier to give. You should try thinking of yourself as a "coach" rather than a "police officer."

Remember: Coaches work with athletes to improve their potential; they are not disciplinarians whose sole role is to find fault.

Next, it may help if you try to imagine what will happen if you refrain from giving the criticism. Avoiding criticism just so that you don't hurt someone's feelings will accomplish nothing—and maybe even make things worse.

It will make it much easier to give criticism if you follow the preparatory steps outlined in the flowchart on page 83. By properly planning in advance, the actual encounter will be far less frightening and unpleasant.

Picking the Right Time

It's not necessary that you criticize a person for something as soon as you find out about it. What's really important is that you talk to the person before a chance occurs to repeat the same mistake. As Susan Taylor, editor-in-chief at *Essence* magazine, says, "If someone is hurting and punishing himself or herself for an error, it may be best to defer giving the criticism until the person has calmed down." Also, as we noted earlier, if you sit down with the person at a less stressful time and discuss when and how he or she prefers to be criticized, it will be easier for you to pick the right time to actually put criticism into practice.

As we noted, timing is a highly personal matter. One interviewee said he likes to be criticized in the morning so that he can begin to work on it right away. Another disagreed, favoring criticism at the end of the day so that he could go home and devise a plan of action undisturbed by the distractions of the office. One person advised to give criticism toward the end of the week so that the person can think about it calmly over the weekend. The human resources director of a telecommunications firm prefers to give criticism early in the week so that the person can begin to correct the problem right away. How do you know what will work best for the receiver you're criticizing? Ask!

Getting Started

There are several ways to preface criticism so that it comes across as less harsh and better intentioned. Rick Sklar, who now owns his own radio consulting firm based in New York, reinforces the positive aspect of his relationship with the receiver by first taking him or her to lunch. Other people remind the receiver of the expectations that both parties have previously established and the goals that they are working toward together.

As an example of how to cushion criticism, Susan Taylor of *Essence* begins by pointing out some positive feature of the person's work. Commenting on an article, for instance, she may tell one of her writers, "The opening is strong and I really think the points you're making come across well, but we have to adjust the tone to fit our readership better. . . ."

To help *yourself* get the criticism session started, you can also try the following quick charges to lower your stress and make yourself feel more comfortable. First, you can perform the "Breathing Quick Charge," as mentioned on page 67. Remember to inhale and exhale slowly and smoothly through your nose. At the same time, relax all your muscles progressively from your head to your toes, trying to create a feeling of calmness throughout your body. It takes only a few seconds, and no one can tell you're doing it.

A second quick charge is the "Memorize Quick-Charge." It involves memorizing your opening statement. Remember that, as the giver, you are in complete control until you actually deliver the criticism. Therefore, you can open the discussion with whatever comment you think will work best. Memorizing the statement in advance will boost your confidence and help you get off to a smooth start.

Yet a third quick charge, the "Matching Quick Charge," involves adopting the other person's nonverbal behavior. For example, if the man sitting across the desk from you has his legs crossed, adopt the same position. If you can, try to adjust your rate of breathing to his as well. Some psychologists believe that doing this is an effective means of literally putting yourself in someone else's shoes, and therefore entering his or her world. According to Kim Kostere, therapist and co-author of *Get the Results You Want: A Systematic Approach to N.L.P.*, "The quickest way to build rapport with someone is to adopt their nonverbal behaviors. It functions like a feed-back loop. The other person is seeing himself or herself from the outside. It creates a feeling of oneness, synchronicity, empathy. One can liken it to dancing in rhythm with a partner instead of being out of step and stubbing each other's toes."

Handling the Exchange

Interviewees suggested that there are a number of giver behaviors that prevent the criticism from being delivered as effectively as it could be. For instance, are any of the following typical of you?

1. Do you tend to give criticism when you are pressed for time?
2. Do you interrupt the receiver when he or she is responding?
3. Do you get easily or visibly upset or angry?
4. Do you have trouble citing specifics?
5. Do you hastily conclude the criticism without giving the receiver ample time or opportunity to reply?

If you know that you are inclined to any of these behaviors, then you have identified certain predictable tendencies, which you must work to overcome. Some of the quick charges we've discussed can help overcome counterproductive, predictable tendencies. To give you practice with timing and implementation, use the mental rehearsal step from the giver's flowchart. For example, if you tend to interrupt the receiver, you can remind yourself, while mentally imagining the situation, to let the person finish before responding. Remember: It's often not the content of the criticism that bothers people but the way it's delivered.

Couching Criticism So It's Helpful

The key word here is "helpful." You may have the noblest intentions in the world, but if the receiver fails to see that you are trying to be helpful, you've lost the battle. Remember, you should criticize others the way *they* prefer to be criticized. For example, Nick used to be blunt when he criticized his secretary, Sally. Afterward, she would sulk, sometimes for days on end. Finally, Nick realized that Sally preferred to be criticized in a softer manner. The next time he had to give her a review, he modified his approach and found that she was much more responsive. He made a potentially uncomfortable situation far more comfortable, and a greater level of trust and respect began to develop between the two as a result.

Another effective means of couching criticism is to use a method based on the receiver's favored mode of learning—primarily visual, auditory, or kinesthetic (see chapter 3). Most people use all three representational modes, but one tends to dominate over the others. For example, if an employee is visually oriented, the giver could say something like, "Greg, I want to clear up some matters with you so that we see eye to eye. The way we're doing things now seem fuzzy and out of focus. . . ." Have you ever addressed a group of people and known that you've expressed yourself clearly, yet some members of the group did not seem to grasp what you said? The problem could well be that your words did not tap into their representational system.

When trying to couch criticism, other decisions about word choice may be equally important. There are certain words that some people are highly sensitive to; I call these "negative stress triggers," and they alone are enough to irritate the receiver. For instance, a male executive who addresses middle-aged women as "girls" may infuriate them. Again, you should try to establish what a person's negative stress triggers are during the preparatory stages, when you're turning unspoken expectations into spoken ones.

Any potential help that the criticism might offer is greatly lost when the giver asks whether or not the receiver understands the criticism and has any questions about it. The question isn't helpful because most people will say to an authority figure who's criticizing them, "Yes, I understand," or "No, I don't have any questions," even when they do. Only an unusually secure person will answer differently. However, to ensure that the receiver has, in fact, understood your message, you may wish to summarize your meeting on paper and jot down the major points. In this way, agreed-on expectations can be managed more closely.

Finally, a key process involved in couching criticism is to be as good a listener as you possibly can. My interviewees reported that, when they are receivers of criticism, nothing causes more stress for them than for the giver not to listen to their comments.

Keeping Criticism from Becoming Personal

To prevent criticism from being taken as a personal affront, it's important that you focus on specific *issues*. You should also monitor the conversation and be aware of whether it's turning into a competitive contest.

Warren, a manager in an engineering firm, had to remove Sam from a project he'd been working on for five months. Warren knew that Sam was highly sensitive to criticism, but the project was not progressing the way Warren felt it should. To avoid personalizing the criticism, Warren used a very simple but effective technique. He drew a circle—knowing that Sam responded best to visual cues—and divided it in half. He then labeled one half "personal" and the other "professional." He began the conversation by emphasizing how well they got along personally as co-workers and the great respect he'd developed for Sam over the years as an engineer and as a human being. He turned to the professional side of the figure and praised Sam for his many past accomplishments. Then Warren brought up the problem, and, because Sam knew that Warren had spoken honestly and respectfully, the issue of the botched project was accepted and acted on far more readily than it might have otherwise.

Not all managers are as adroit or perceptive as Warren, however, and tempers may flare during such unpleasant confrontations. If this should occur, here are a couple of tips and quick charges you can use to help defuse the situation:

1. Pause. Take a sip of water or do something else to slow down the momentum of the conversation.

2. Change the subject and talk about something far removed from the matter at hand. For instance, you might turn around for a brief moment, look out the window, and then swiftly switch subjects. The swift, yet abrupt, introduction of a new subject will surprise the other person and temporarily create amnesia.

3. Do the "breathing quick charge" exercise described on page 67. As we noted there, this exercise helps relax you and decreases your tension.

THE FOLLOW-UP PHASE

At the close of the criticism session, you need to discuss the type of action desired and develop an agreement to implement that action. (As we observed in chapter 5, if the receiver is unable to take direct action on the criticism, he or she is likely to feel frustrated or suspicious of the giver's motives.) Built into the agreement is a "follow-up" on the part of the giver to take notice of the person's progress. For example, Shelley, an office manager, may call in one of the secretaries from a secretarial pool and say, "Linda, I think you work well with everyone and your work is valued, but very often people will see you sitting at your desk reading the newspaper or making personal calls when a lot of important projects are not being worked on."

Linda explains that her work load is very erratic: sometimes she'll have nothing to do but answer the phone; then all of a sudden she'll be given three projects marked "Rush." Together they identify and establish the source of the problem. Shelley and Linda then worked out a system of prioritizing tasks. "A" tasks have to be done right away, "B"s should be done right away if there are no "A"s and so on. They also agree that if Linda finds herself overwhelmed with too many projects at once, she has the authority to hire a temp for the day to help her out. The two parties further agree to have a regularly scheduled monthly follow-up meeting to discuss whether the work is flowing properly, and whether a temp is being utilized effectively.

When the follow-up stage is implemented successfully, there are bonuses:

1. The receiver feels a sense of accomplishment—it's easy to recognize when agreements have been kept.

2. Self-confidence is strengthened further when the manager follows up and takes notice of any progress.

3. The receiver is more likely to accept the consequences if the agreement is not kept because the conditions were spelled out from the beginning. The giver is simply carrying out what was originally discussed.

Improving Behavior Without Criticism

As we've seen, there are many situations in which criticism, well timed and thoughtfully presented and delivered, can have a strong positive impact on performance. However, direct criticism need not be the only way to influence behavior. There are several creative *indirect* methods you can use.

Mirroring

Mirroring is a very useful technique for altering someone's behavior. Let's go back to our example of Linda and the office manager, Shelley. Instead of criticizing Linda for failing to utilize her time well and causing projects to fall off schedule, Shelley invites Linda out to lunch one day and casually says, "You know, some days I get overwhelmed. Linda, you regularly have to handle several people's work load. How do *you* deal with this?" With this approach, Shelley opens up the idea of prioritizing projects. The mirroring technique is valuable because it avoids confrontation. The criticism is disguised when you present it as if it were your own problem or somebody else's. Therefore, the actual receiver (Linda) saves face by being placed in a position of working with the giver to resolve an issue. The two parties can now easily keep the conversation focused on content issues and not personality conflicts. As a result, pride and self-confidence are restored or even boosted, and the receiver is less likely to respond defensively than if the criticism was offered directly.

Referral

In this approach, the giver brings in a qualified third party whose style and/or level of authority may be better suited to working with the receiver.

An example that we can relate to is the father who decides to teach his teenage son to drive. The only problem is that every time the father points out what the son is doing wrong, he personalizes it and an argument ensues. In order to avoid these seemingly unavoidable conflicts, the father hires a professional instructor. Though pointing out the same problems and deficiencies addressed by the father, the instructor's "advice" seems less like criticism and is more easily accepted because of the instructor's assumed expertise and the absence of any prior history of arguing with the boy.

An example of a more subtle approach using the referral technique: Ted is a creative type who has been making repeated mistakes on a recently assigned editorial project. Rather than directly criticizing him, the supervisor schedules a progress update meeting and during the meeting discusses the particular project in question. As relevant ideas get raised, the supervisor suggests that Ted continue the conversation with Phil, someone who has demonstrated expertise in the area under consideration.

Similar principles may be operating when organizations bring in outside consultants to revamp departments or recommend other improvements. "I tried to say the same thing you did," bewildered managers often tell these consultants, "and everyone just ignored me." The referral approach provides the giver with another effective way to direct behavior toward desired end results without having to actually confront the receiver.

We've now examined both sides of the criticism process, exploring what it's like to be a receiver and a giver. What ensures that the criticism will be positively received and that action will be taken? For instance, have you ever wondered how it is that a coach can scream at a football player on the sidelines during a game and all the while have the player nod his head in agreement and then return to the playing field energized and ready to play ball?

What's behind the coach's screaming and the player's nodding is a strong degree of acceptance coupled with mutually agreed-on expectations—the foundations of the criticism process.

COMMUNICATING EXPECTATIONS: PAVING THE WAY FOR SUCCESSFUL CRITICISM

Establishing mutually agreed-on expectations provides a foundation of common understanding between the giver and the receiver on which the criticism can be built and accepted.

Because of its significance, let's explore what expectations are, and how they help to define certain aspects of a relationship.

To begin with, an expectation is defined as the mental anticipation that someone will behave in a certain way. We may distinguish between two types of expectations. *Spoken expectations,* as the term suggests, are explicitly communicated from one party to another. For example, after joining an organization, a new employee is usually *told* what to expect in the way of job responsibilities, salary, health-insurance benefits, vacation and holidays, and so on. If early violations of expressed rules are met with criticism, the employee knows why. (Some firms present this information in a personnel manual or handbook.)

On the other hand, organizations also have *unspoken* expectations, which are *not* overtly expressed. A new employee who violates one of these could react in a perplexed or confused way when an unspoken expectation is violated. Examples of unspoken organizational expectations and how they operate include the following:

1. In many industries, people who rise to the top managerial positions typically come from sales or marketing, even though there are many equally intelligent and qualified people in the technical areas. The unspoken expectation is that those who are not from sales or marketing will have to put in extra effort to prove themselves.

2. Many organizations that have no dress code show favoritism to men and women who dress well. They are the ones who are more likely to be advanced. The unspoken expectation? If you want to get ahead, look good!

3. Seriously overweight people are rarely promoted to high-ranking positions. Unspoken expectation? Stay thin and advance.

4. In some firms, although there is no official antismoking policy, certain departments or divisions consist exclusively of nonsmokers. Unspoken expectation: Don't smoke.

5. In many companies, employees and bosses go out for a couple of drinks after work; employees who don't go along somehow get bypassed when promotions are handed out. Unspoken

expectation: Be part of the after-five crowd—even though you don't drink.

6. If an employee gets out of line or too drunk at an office party, whether during work hours or not, his or her potential for a promotion or other advancement may be seriously jeopardized. Unspoken expectation: It's better not to drink than to show any loss of control.

As you are well aware, there is a prevailing attitude toward criticism in any given company. Joe O'Brien, who heads up the educational division of PGA of America, points out that there are several signals you can use to assess an organization's attitude toward criticism. These include:

1. Is there a sense among managers and employees that honest feedback (including criticism) is given fairly?

2. Does the salary schedule tie in with the performance review?

3. Is a manager assessed on the progress and development of his or her people, and is this assessment included in performance reviews?

4. Is the performance review conducted more frequently than the traditional once a year?

Joyce Daza, head of safety and management training at a New York telecommunications firm, goes on to say that she believes that a company's review policy is a key gauge of its attitude toward criticism. Many firms, she points out, use the annual review chiefly as a disciplinary measure. She also feels that it is important to look at whether the organization conducts training programs on effective feedback on criticism or whether employees are left to train at the "school of hard knocks."

On an individual level, managers should know that employees often have unspoken expectations of their own when they start a new job. A young college graduate who takes an entry-level clerical job at an international bank, for instance, may imagine this position as just a temporary stepping-stone on the way to an executive spot, while the reality of the situation may be quite different. This position, in fact, may have no planned career path at all!

Unspoken expectations can cause problems at home as well as at work. A classic case involved Jeannine and Tony, husband and wife. Both Jeannine and Tony held full-time jobs. Jeannine would often hurry home half an hour earlier than Tony, freshen up, and change into a more comfortable outfit in anticipation of greeting Tony. Upon Tony's arrival, she would hope for a kiss and a hug; each time she was disappointed. Tony would open the door, say "Hello," drop his briefcase, hang up his coat, and then sit in the living room and read the paper. Jeannine, feeling miffed and rejected, would clatter about in the kitchen as she prepared dinner, slamming pots and pans to vent her annoyance. Sometimes Tony would hear the racket and ask her whether anything was wrong. Jeannine just said no.

Finally fed up, she *asked* him for a kiss when she met him at the door. Tony responded by saying, "Gee, good idea, why didn't I think of that?" A tradition began. Jeannine learned that her earlier frustrations could easily have been averted by a simple request.

Many of us play a variety of games, both on the job and off, in which we think we are making our wants known but actually do so in a form of code—e.g., Jeannine's standing at the door—that another person does not always recognize or decode correctly. The trick is to turn *unspoken* expectations into *spoken* ones. It's as simple as that.

The exchange of expectations is a form of communicating information to avoid guesswork about what people expect from one another. If expectations are clarified and agreed on in advance, energy can be directed in ways that will be more productive and rewarding.

As in a case where expectations *were* conveyed, consider a young man, Fred, who was hired by the distinguished architect I. M. Pei. Pei felt that Fred was enormously talented and creative, with the potential to be an exceptional architect in his own right. But when Fred joined Pei's firm, he found that none of his colleagues paid much attention to his visionary ideas. "Oh, you're just a dreamer, Fred" became a common remark at staff meetings.

The problem was Fred's appearance. With his long hair and

exuberant clothes, Fred seemed as flamboyant as some of his suggestions. Finally, I. M. Pei himself took Fred aside after one meeting. He put an arm around his protégé's shoulder and said in a cordial but firm tone, "You know, Fred, what good are your ideas if no one is willing to listen to them only because of the way you look." Fred got the message—Pei's almost fatherly approach helped soften the blow—and he began to dress more appropriately.

A few weeks later, Christmas bonuses were handed out. Fred hadn't been with the firm long enough to qualify for a real bonus, but Pei came by and slipped him $300 and suggested he put it toward a new suit. Pei thus positively reinforced his communication of expectations, and, in time, Fred became one of the most highly valued architects in the firm. Did Fred become a conformist? Yes, because he wanted to succeed and yielded to the expectation.

This incident exemplifies a perceptive, sensitive way of turning unspoken expectations into spoken ones, as well as of criticizing someone in a positive way that yielded positive results— improving Fred's performance in the organization. Pei was able to point out how Fred's personal career goals could be brought into sync with the objectives of the organization.

There are several advantages, in addition to what we've already discussed, to establishing clear, mutually agreed-on expectations:

1. There is a greater probability that the receiver will approve criticism and act on it because expectations are understood and objectives are shared.

2. The receiver is much less likely to personalize the criticism if it is recognized that it was delivered in accordance with the expectations agreed upon at the outset.

Establishing the foundation of mutually agreed-on expectations extends to working relationships—how best to work together. For instance, when an employee first enters a new job, a supervisor usually provides guidance regarding job responsibilities and benefits. But once the employee gets into the swing of the job, situations may arise that don't quite fit into the preestablished mold. People often receive unfair criticism because there are aspects of the job no one told them about. Within relationships, a number of expectations exist about the way we want to be treated. Take, as an example, what is expected after a task is delegated. Some people work best if they are left alone to complete the assignment. Such employees are likely to be unnerved or frustrated if the boss keeps coming around to see how the project is progressing; they wonder whether the boss believes they are really capable of doing the work. On the other hand, there are also people who feel that the boss isn't interested in them or their work if there is no interaction once the task has been assigned. A truly effective manager will discuss these different styles with each employee.

Another sensitive work-related expectation is how a person should be rewarded for work well done. In one particularly interesting case, Miranda, a trader at a large New York brokerage firm, put in a huge amount of overtime while her boss, Karl, was overseas on a lengthy business trip. Besides handling her own accounts, she managed his. When Karl returned to New York, he told Miranda he appreciated all her efforts and as a token of his appreciation he gave her a beautifully engraved Cartier bracelet.

In one sense, Miranda was delighted, but she was also terribly disappointed because what she really wanted was time off. For days afterward, she walked around the office with a sullen look. Karl noticed the change in her behavior, but decided to say nothing.

Karl really isn't an insensitive man; he just failed to openly communicate expectations. He assumed that he knew how to best reward Miranda.

This is a rather dramatic example of how differing expectations about appropriate rewards may cause conflict, but this is a rather common source of tension. Some employees want raises or bonuses for work well done; others want a better title or increased responsibilities; still others want a larger office. Some seek verbal praise and visibility, while others find mere words an unacceptable substitute for higher pay or other tangible rewards. When one large midwestern company had to freeze salaries, it interviewed its administrative staff to find out how the organization could still let its people know they were appreciated. The most commonly appreciated gestures were simply being thanked, being taken to lunch, or being sent flowers. Rewards need not always be elaborate, but they should be appropriate to the person's goals and preferences whenever possible.

Just as important as understanding how people prefer to be praised is understanding how they prefer to be criticized. Do not run the risk of falsely assuming that other people are just like you. It's imperative that you find out how they want criticism to be directed to them.

Here are several steps you can take:

1. Select a good time. Make sure you have enough time for an uninterrupted conversation. It's best if you select an unstressed moment—say, on a slow day when neither of you has a great deal to do, or possibly over a friendly lunch.

2. To open the conversation: a good way is to ask whether the person expects to make any mistakes by the end of the first year and, if so, explore how he or she would prefer to be criticized for them. For further clarification, ask whether they are more responsive to criticism that's direct and to the point or softer and more cushioned.

3. Identify when it's best to criticize. Find out *when* they are most receptive to criticism—say, early versus late in the day or week. (Interviewees revealed a wide range of preferences on this topic: for example, some said, "Never before a major event.")

4. Determine particular stress producers. Find out the circumstances under which criticism will most certainly antagonize the person. Some individuals resent being criticized in public. Still others are especially sensitive to certain words or phrases. One way to identify this information is to simply ask whether anyone has ever criticized the person so that the conversation turned into an argument. If the person can't think of someone, then ask if there is someone whose criticism he or she felt particularly comfortable with. Try to find out what that person said or did.

5. Improve communications. Obviously, it's important that the message be clearly understood. As we've mentioned before, to

improve communications find out how the person learns best. Some of us learn best by *listening*—attending lectures, listening to audio tapes, talking to someone. Other people learn better by *looking*—e.g., reading, watching films, or studying illustrations. Still others learn best by *doing*; this is what we would call a hands-on approach.

To help you assess how someone learns best, pay attention to the words that are used. As an easy exercise, ask the person to describe what it's like to be on a beach at sunset. If the person is visual, he or she will use primarily visual imagery: "The sun is red in the sky"; "The palm trees are swaying." If the person responds best to auditory stimuli, words will be selected that relate to auditory imagery: "The leaves rustle in the breeze"; "A sea bird cries out." And a hands-on type will use kinesthetic language: "The sand feels warm against my feet"; "The breeze caresses my skin." Few of us are exclusively auditory, visual, or kinesthetic; most of us are a combination of the three but use one mode predominantly.

6. Be a good listener. Whatever else you do or don't do, it is essential that you *listen* attentively to the person. A quick activity you can perform to prove the importance of being a good listener is to take thirty seconds and identify the three best listeners you know. Do you dislike any of these people? Probably not. We tend to like people whom we perceive to be good listeners.

DEVELOPING MUTUAL EXPECTATIONS

Congruency of goals and objectives provides the foundation on which criticism is built. The more there exists a congruence in a relationship, the greater will be the effective receptivity to criticism.

It is the responsibility of both the giver and the receiver to develop mutual expectations and agreements about various key components that help to define the relationship: clarification of goals, work tasks, quality of work and the working relationship.

Let's go back to the coach and the athlete. The athlete easily handles the coach's criticism because both are working toward one mutually agreed-on goal. They know what is required to achieve the goal.

The coach's yelling is tolerated because at some point in their relationship, it was explained and understood that screaming is linked to belief in the athlete.

Believing in someone is a very important component to building a strong and trusting relationship. Too many of us worry about being accepted, especially when we are being criticized. For the one who is the receiver of criticism, it's easy to interpret what is being said as personal rejection. When this happens, receptivity to criticism decreases and the chances of taking corrective action become unpredictable. For instance, it's unlikely that any positive action will result when someone says, "What's the use? No matter what I do, I'll never please him." However, when strong acceptance exists in relationships, it's much easier to view criticism as nonthreatening and to take corrective action.

When little congruency exists in relationships, not only will the likelihood of criticism increase because of numerous misunderstandings, but the receptivity to criticism and the willingness to take action greatly decreases. Instead of criticism helping to strengthen the relationship, it will help to tear it down. Hostility, fear, disrespect, and anger will take the place of positive feelings associated with a trusting and caring relationship.

THE CONGRUENCY MODEL

A good way to explore what we've been talking about is to look at the *congruency model*. This model represents the interactive relationship that exists between two people. It's a valuable visual aid because at quick glance individuals can easily clarify their relationship with another person, while at the same time learn about the likelihood of that person perceiving criticism as a positive force.

One way to use the model to help clarify relationships is to have individuals separately color in the amount of personal acceptance they feel toward one another and the degree to which they share goals and other expectations that help to define the relationship. The greater the shading in each category, the higher the level of acceptance and the greater the congruency.

As an example, let's say Jane reports to Sandra. Sandra wants to clarify how Jane perceives their relationship. During a time when they are in a receptive mood, both women decide to complete the model separately by coloring in those areas where they feel acceptance exists both professionally and personally, and the degree to which they share mutual expectations.

THE CONGRUENCY MODEL

Separating the personal from the professional aspect of a working relationship is important. Too many of us are worried about being personally liked. While this is indeed desirable, what really matters is that we respect the people we work with as professionals. We've all heard comments like "My doctor's one cold fish, but you couldn't ask for a better surgeon" or "Jack has a huge ego, but he really is the best player we have." Our model captures this distinction. It also helps to visually clarify people's concern about acceptance and rejection.

It also addresses the importance of mutual expectations. As we've said, criticism is more likely to occur when expectations have not been clearly communicated at the beginning. When expectations are mutually understood and accepted, criticism can be more easily tolerated and acted upon.

Chapter 7

HANDLING CRITICISM OFF THE JOB

Work and home aren't the same.

At first glance that may seem obvious. However, looking at the two entities from the perspective of criticism reveals some interesting differences that could easily be overlooked.

At home, relationships are more open. Family members feel they can "let their hair down"—after all, they're at home. In other words, we feel we don't have to be as polite as we are at work or in school. Our behavior is more casual.

Unspoken expectations thrive in families. One such unspoken expectation is that we have to accept a certain level of frustration in dealing with one another. After all, we are not perfect and we don't all think and act alike. At work, when frustration levels peak, depending upon our position, we can leave the job or we can fire the people who work with us.

It's not that simple at home. First, we can't fire our kids (something many parents have probably wished they could do). We can terminate a marriage, but that's an extremely traumatic experience, and the stress that a separation or divorce produces is evidence that we place far more importance on marriage than on employment. After all, you don't have to love your job, we're told, you just work there.

116

What also contributes to the difference between work and home is that at home, we know everyone better and relationships run deeper than they do at work. This provides fertile ground for criticism to thrive.

Add to all of this the fact that at home we rarely take time to discuss openly how to criticize one another, as we do at work. Many organizations have established policies and procedures that clearly describe how managers and employees can best approach giving criticism. Guidelines are frequently written on performance reviews to assist the manager. Management courses are taught for the sole purpose of showing managers how to give criticism effectively. Many organizations even have clear-cut grievance procedures designed to protect employees from being unjustly criticized. Have you ever heard of such well-defined approaches existing in families?

Yet, research indicates that most of us receive more criticism at home than we do at work. Sometimes we wonder whether it is worth handling criticism at work during the day only to have to come home to get more practice at night.

Intentions are not always clear at home either. After all, if one partner has had a rough day at work, the criticisms given at home might not take the other person's best interest into account. Quite the contrary. Instead, the main purpose of the criticism is to let the giver unload some of the day's frustrations.

While issues of respect and self-esteem are a primary concern at work, at home complex issues of love, trust, and commitment are involved. Criticism can matter more at home than it does at work. Work and home domains are different. The home domain consists of several different subspheres—spouses, children, friends, and so on. We shall explore the role of criticism in these subspheres; let's consider marriage first.

MARRIAGE AND CRITICISM

Albert Ellis, the internationally acclaimed founder of rational-emotive therapy, has commented that hostility, not sexual difficulty, is the main reason for bad marriages, and that hostility is aggravated by criticism.

Criticism and the hostility it engenders are often the result of unspoken expectations that exist between partners at the onset of a marriage. Many couples enter into marriage unaware that one or more unspoken expectations are operating. For instance, when we get married, we are supposed to love one another. The underlying expectation is that we are not supposed to criticize each other.

Closely related is the expectation that, because a couple is married, they should treat each other kindly. It's almost as if we feel that kindness is owed to us at home, whereas at work, we have to do something of value to earn it. It's easy to see that if these unspoken expectations are never challenged, a spouse may become horrified and shattered when his or her mate dares to be critical.

Another interesting unspoken expectation that flourishes untested in marriages is the "say-and-do-anything" belief. At work, we can't simply tell everyone exactly how we honestly feel. But at home, we not only feel that we can be honest, but that we can say whatever we want. If we combine this condition with the fact that couples know a great deal about each other, it becomes understandable why spouses receive more criticism from one another than from anyone else.

When couples criticize each other, what's often missing is proper preparation on the part of the giver. No wonder so many people resent being criticized by their spouses. And partners operate as if they have a license to criticize each other.

Traditional Sex Roles

"Criticism is often the result of one partner's attempt to control the other," says Dr. Gwendolyn Grolsby Grant, a New Jersey–based consultant and psychologist. After examining her own relationship as well as working with thousands of men and women nationwide, she found that men typically criticize their wives to control them and to persuade them to return to their traditional roles. This makes husbands feel more comfortable and helps them avoid what Dr. Grant calls the "Greek chorus." The Greek chorus consists of friends, children, and other family members who constantly sing out various messages to keep couples in line. They ask, "How can you let your spouse travel so much? Isn't that kind of risky?"; "You mean to tell me that *you* cook dinner? Never thought I'd see the day when you had an apron on in the kitchen"; and on and on and on.

Wives are berated by the Greek chorus, too. Typically, they'll hear messages like "Aren't you neglecting your family when you work all day?"; "Do you think it's wise to travel so much? I mean, doesn't your husband get lonely? Who cooks dinner for him if you're out evenings?" Or "You're working so hard. Why doesn't your husband do the cooking?"

Baby-boomers grew up with the traditional belief that men are "breadwinners." Dr. Grant says that the key word to focus on is "winners." Men are the winners, and if they sense they lack control in a relationship, they interpret it as "losing." So men often use criticism for the purpose of gaining control and therefore "winning." They don't really intend to find fault with their partners, simply to assert control.

One likely arena in which men feel threatened with losing is financial, Dr. Grant points out. "Remember men were 'bread' winners. The slang term 'bread' doesn't restrict itself to putting food on the table—it also refers to bringing in *money*. With increasing numbers of women entering the marketplace today and earning substantial salaries, men more than ever before have had to contend with the fact that they are no longer always winners. That in and of itself," says Dr. Grant, "can be a great threat to the man and cause him to sense that he's losing. What's ironic about our modern society is that the 'traditional woman' men are supposed to be living with is nonexistent," continues Dr. Grant. "Men need supportive women. Being supportive doesn't mean jumping through hoops regularly. Instead, it means having a kind of strength that is focused on achieving the goals and dreams that both parties share. Men *think* they need to be in control. But they actually need to have a partner who assists them with handling today's pressures."

It's important to keep in mind that we are not discussing here whether such attitudes are right or wrong, good or bad. That's not our focus. We are trying to understand those special circumstances that exist in loving relationships that breed criticism.

Frequently, spouses will use criticism as a way to find out whether they are still loved. The unspoken message is "If you love me, you'll handle me in ways that will let me know you love me."

Let's apply this insight to Sally and Dick. When Dick tells Sally, "Don't be late, the way you usually are. Let's meet here no later than six," Sally has the choice of perceiving his comment as a matter of fact or as a criticism. How would she handle the situation if she perceives his comment as criticism?

Sally would be wise to consider using the receiver's flowchart on page 29. Sally follows each step of the flowchart until she reaches the steps assessing the intention of the criticism and her understanding of it. Dick's critical statement lacks specificity and he has exaggerated, Sally decides. Sally knows that she is occasionally late, but she is not chronically so, as Dick has indicated. Because she questions the accuracy of the criticism, Sally decides to go back and reexamine its intent. The intent *could* have been to keep Sally in line and direct her behavior back to a more traditional role. Or it could have been that he was in a bad mood. Sally discounts that option because it was too early in the day to attribute the bad mood to any specific situation. Third, it could be a clue that something is bothering him. Sally has learned from living with Dick that sometimes he'll criticize her constantly for little things. This situation is analogous to water dripping on a rock. No one drop will cause much damage. Instead, it's the accumulation of many drops over a period of time that causes the rock to show signs of wear and tear. But Sally senses this isn't the answer either. He hasn't bombarded her with a series of criticisms. She concludes that the purpose of the criticism is to remind her of her traditional role.

Just taking a few moments to sort out the intention behind the criticism and her understanding of it helps to keep Sally from becoming frustrated, as she did in the past. Previously, when Dick would criticize Sally, her stress level would quickly reach explosive levels. She compounded her stress because not only was she uncomfortable with what Dick said, but she was even more upset over the way he would criticize her. She would think to herself, "He shouldn't criticize me like that. He knows how negatively it affects me. How dare he! Especially after I told him how it hurts." The consequences were also stressful because Sally would start to doubt herself. Even though Dick would exaggerate, there usually was a grain of truth in it that would compound itself in Sally's mind.

After much work and continued effort, Sally is better able to see Dick as he really is. When she views him objectively, she is able to see that he exaggerates most situations, whether at home or work. Instead of resenting the way he behaves, she simply thinks, "Wouldn't it be nice if he would say, 'Don't worry if you get home late. I can start dinner.'" Sally also has worked at interpreting what Dick says as neutral information. Doing this gives Sally the control she needs to use the flowchart effectively.

Continuing to work with the flowchart, Sally quickly asks herself whether Dick's criticism has any constructive value. She decides that its only true purposes are to let her know that Dick is feeling uncomfortable and that she needs to be sensitive to that, along with the point that honoring their agreement to be on time is something they both value. Most importantly, Sally asks herself what kind of action she should take. To deal with this question appropriately, Sally has learned that she needs to ask herself what she wants. Determining *specifically* what we want points each of us in the direction that we desire.

In Sally's case, she decides that she wants to go to her aerobics class and run errands on the way home. She also decides to apprise Dick of the situation. When she gets to the office, she dials Dick's number. When he comes to the phone, Sally says, "Sweetheart, I'll do my best to be home by six, but let me tell you my schedule. I've got to make two stops on the way home. First, I have to go to the supermarket to pick up the roast and the other groceries for tonight, and then I need to go to the cleaner's. I'll plan on being home between six and six-fifteen."

Dick says, "Fine, Sally, see you when you get home. Have a great day. 'Bye, sweetheart."

Let's review what Sally did.

When the intent behind the criticism is to encourage the spouse to return to a more traditional role, whether it's by picking on him or her ("The dinner two weeks ago was too bland") or using little put-downs, it's valuable for the partner receiving the criticism to practice what Sally did.

1. Start the response with some verbal stroking. When Sally phoned Dick, she said, "Sweetheart, I'll do my best to be home by six." The advantage to this approach is twofold. First, it defuses any hostility that may exist between partners without being manipulative in any sort of negative way. The receiver is accurately assessing the intention of the criticism and responding to the wants and needs of the giver. She is expressing her love in a way that her mate understands. Second, it puts into practice Dr. Grant's philosophy: "Say things that you want them to say to you." After Dr. Grant explained her philosophy to me, I tried it on my husband, because we are both strong people and we do not lead traditional lives. From firsthand experience, I can assure you that it helps. It might be something you'd like to try.

2. When necessary, be supportive by being part of the solution.

HANDLING ARGUMENTS

As might be expected, arguments can easily crop up when partners engage in criticism. After all, criticism is negative and people generally don't like it. Our spouses are no exception.

When an argument arises, make sure that it doesn't turn into another source of criticism, as in "All you want to do is argue," or "I can't believe we're always arguing." Such statements can fuel even more arguments, especially because the woman will tend, according to the findings from Simmons/Bright, to personalize the criticism more than the man will. This could be related to the socialization process that men go through when they are boys. They play games to win; they are not as concerned about hurt feelings and personal likes and dislikes. As an avid male basketball player once told me, "When I played college basketball, I couldn't stand some of the players on the team. But that was okay. We just wanted to win the title." Women in general tend not to share these experiences.

Here are some ideas to keep in mind the next time an argument flares up with someone with whom you are close:

It's Okay to Argue

It helps to bring things to the surface. This is important because, as the survey revealed, couples tend to wait until tension builds to the breaking point.

However, there are two ways to argue: A constructive or productive way and a free-for-all destructive way. These were well described by authors Dr. George R. Bach and Peter Wyden in 1970 in their book *The Intimate Enemy*. The authors likened the constructive way of arguing to being in a boxing ring where both partners arc wearing "boxing gloves." Both boxing partners agree that hitting is restricted to certain parts of the body. In this setting, it's almost as if partners dance with one another in the ring as they fight. But the other way to fight, which is destructive, is analogous to a street fight, where "anything goes"—stones, brass knuckles, knives. The important distinction here lies in the consequences that ensue. Remember, hurt feelings, like bruises, cut deep and when partners fight with no holds barred, the recovery period is consequently much longer.

Be Prepared

Be prepared for an immediate reaction after criticizing your partner. After all, criticism is negative, so it's not unusual for the receiver to react defensively.

As the giver, you should not be shocked by this response; to cast judgment of any sort at this point is unfair. Pause for a few moments to let things calm down before responding.

Keep the Big Picture in Focus

When arguing, it's important for someone to step back and view your disagreement in light of a bigger picture. For instance, to help objectify the situation, it's helpful to wonder how important this situation will be five years from now. It's also helpful if you label arguments according to their importance. For instance, we all experience five-cent arguments and dollar arguments. The five-cent arguments are probably the ones that get triggered when we criticize someone because we're tired or irritable. In the final analysis, these things may have little or no value. Bach and Wyden called these arguments "fighting over trivia."

One of the reasons couples tend to get upset over nothing, said Bach and Wyden, is because lovers care a great deal about each other. Lovers will continually test each other's temper or their "good" and "bad" nature. It's almost as if they hold hypotheses about each other that, like scientific research, have to be checked out periodically. Bach and Wyden believe that "this is an intuitive technique and a constructive one as long as it is not overdone in [an] exaggerated, vindictive manner."

They also attribute trivia fighting to "gunnysacking." When we fill up our gunnysack, it doesn't take much to cause it to spill over. If, as the results of the Simmons/Bright nationwide study suggest, people do tend to wait until the tension builds before criticizing, it's likely that criticism causes many arguments. So be sure to remember to sort out whether it's a five-cent argument or a dollar one.

Ten-Dollar Arguments

Ten-dollar arguments are the ones worth investing in because they deal with more important issues. For instance, a husband may criticize his wife for working nights. Or a wife may criticize her husband for bringing home work-related reading material. Or the golf pro may be criticized for not spending enough time with the family during the summer months. These are core issues related to one's work and home lives, and they need to be discussed. It's worth the investment of time and energy. What constitutes a ten-dollar argument versus a five-cent argument may vary from one couple to another. However, what won't differ is that all arguments are not five-cent ones. You need to establish the value of the argument.

Be prepared to listen. Interviewees in the study repeatedly said that, when they were receivers of criticism, one thing that bothered them the most was that the giver was a poor listener.

Listening to your partner is extremely important. People, especially your spouse, need to feel they are important. When you listen without interrupting, it communicates that you value what they have to say. If a partner remains silent, you should not automatically interpret this as agreement, disagreement, or uncooperativeness. The silence may indicate the ability to listen without interruption.

Keep the "three wants" in mind. Stay focused on what you want before, during, and after the argument. Keep in mind that in any situation you have numerous "wants." For convenience's sake, these typically fall into three categories: end result wants; process wants; and postsituation wants. End result wants refer to the end goal that you are hoping to achieve. Process wants are related to the means needed to achieve the end goal. Postsituation wants cover the aftermath of attaining the goal.

It's valuable to determine clearly all three wants when arguing. The reasons are obvious. For some of us, they are so obvious that we take them for granted. Understanding the wants helps you to stay focused on resolving the issue at hand. Too often we let the argument degenerate into who's "right" and who's "wrong." There's no need to remind you that in such situations you can win the battle but lose the war.

Determining your wants also helps to keep the quality of the argument on a higher level. The combatants are more inclined to listen to one another instead of constantly interrupting to express their own views of the situation. They take a more active interest in learning about the other person's point of view, thereby discovering more easily where they disagree, and they are better able to stick to the subject at hand and not personalize the argument.

Determining wants also makes it possible to know how and when to end an argument. How many times have we prolonged an argument way beyond the point of its being effective? Knowing when you reach that point and knowing how to handle it require control or self-management.

MANAGING YOURSELF FOR GREATER CONTROL

When arguing with your spouse or anyone else, it's important to manage yourself effectively. It's important to keep in mind specific "personal management wants." This means being selective in your choice of words and managing your stress level so you don't lose your temper. Arguments are fueled by our lack of ability to control ourselves appropriately.

Try to remember to speak slowly. As stress levels rise, our rate of speech generally accelerates. Speaking slowly will help you keep your own stress level and the momentum generated by the argument itself under better control, thus enabling you to maintain a proper focus.

An Argument Recovery Program

Once the dust settles, how can couples avoid letting the same argument resurface in one week, in two weeks, or even five years from now? By trying to establish an effective argument recovery program.

One approach many use successfully involves using the Dual Garbage Disposal Quick Charge. Both partners practice the technique. When they sense that the argument has lost some of its steam, one of them should ask, "Is there anything we need to discuss further, or can we empty this into the garbage disposal?" If the other partner feels that there is more to talk about, this is the time to bring it out into the open. It helps to avoid gunnysacking. Each partner should agree to continue the discussion or, if preferable, to decide on a specific place and time to talk further. If both partners agree that there is nothing further to discuss, then the whole argument is placed into the garbage disposal. One of the advantages to using this quick charge is that it helps to eliminate the kinds of arguments that go on repeatedly for years. Couples need to learn from their arguments and then let them go.

Now that the argument is over, it is important for the couple to "make up." Besides being the "best part of the argument," it also nurtures the relationship. Here are some interesting recovery approaches that you and your spouse might like to try:

One couple I interviewed hold hands to signify the recovery stage of their arguments. Another uses a sort of growling sound to signal that a truce is in the making. If one partner makes a growling sound and the other spouse returns a similar sound or smile, they know they have successfully reached a truce.

Using fictitious characters works well in helping couples reunite comfortably and playfully. Consider John and Mary, who've been married for six years. John flies off the handle easily, but Mary is unaccustomed to being around emotional people and she often hints to John that she wishes he would learn to control himself better.

John, however, has quite the opposite opinion. He believes that it is healthy to "let it all out." That way he avoids bottling up his emotions—which he felt his father did. His father died of a heart attack when he was fifty-one.

John and Mary worked out a creative solution to their dilemma by inventing a fictitious character whom they call Mr. Mouth.

They both agreed on this name because Mr. Mouth didn't have the negative connotation that, say, Mr. Temper would have had. After John had lost his temper and things had calmed down a bit, he or Mary would make a casual reference to "Mr. Mouth," saying something like "There goes Mr. Mouth again. Boy, he's been around a lot lately. I wonder whether there is anything else Mr. Mouth wants to say so I can get back to my book." The presence of Mr. Mouth, as you can see, helps to defuse personal attacks while providing each partner with a vehicle to talk about their problems in a more detached manner. Mr. Mouth becomes a fictitious but effective scapegoat.

Such techniques may seem silly to an outsider looking in, but to the couple the message is clear: they have clearly established an agreed-upon recovery approach that they can both comfortably use to let go of the argument and simultaneously to reinforce their relationship.

When Silence Is Appropriate

Sometimes arguments result when one partner thinks that it's best to be totally honest with the other. In such cases, one partner may repeatedly point out a mate's negative aspects, which the other person perceives as criticism. Is it best to be totally honest? Or is it better to remain silent at times?

Generally, it is good to be honest, but not if the sole purpose is honesty just for its own sake. If this is the case, the person may not be keeping the receiver's best interests in mind by constantly reciting his or her strengths and weaknesses. In fact, this approach may do more harm than good.

Many negative things are insignificant in terms of the big picture. For instance, if a spouse squeezes the toothpaste from the middle of the tube instead of the end, or leaves dirty clothes scattered around the house, or repeatedly forgets where a pair of glasses are, how important are these things in the big picture—individually or collectively? Keeping the big picture in focus when you deal with day-to-day issues helps to keep things in proper perspective.

If someone constantly berates his or her spouse about little things, it becomes very difficult for the receiver to differentiate important criticism from less significant criticism. If a partner is criticized in the same way for every action, he or she begins to minimize the importance of all criticism, in much the same way that an employee may neglect the truly high-priority project when the boss continually insists that every job is top priority. After a while, the giver will get labeled as a "chronic critiholic" and is no longer taken seriously by his or her spouse or other family members. (More about critiholics in chapter 8.)

Ironically, sometimes when we habitually criticize our spouses, the more defensive and resistant to change he or she will become and the very quality or behavior we dislike is only reinforced.

As a classic example of this situation, consider Don and Janet. Janet constantly criticizes Don for watching too much television. Janet told me, "We both work all day and as soon as Don gets home, I start preparing dinner and Don turns on the TV. We never talk. The only time we speak to one another is during the commercials. I can't stand it."

Let's listen in on a typical early-evening conversation:

JANET: Don, do you have to watch TV? We never talk. Can't we just sit together and communicate for a change? All you do is watch that stupid box. I hate it.

DON: I like watching TV when I get home—it's relaxing.

JANET: But, Don, I've been working all day and I need to relax, too. We just never communicate anymore.

DON (*his patience is wearing thin*): You know why I watch TV every night? So I won't have to put up with your constant nagging.

It's at this point that Janet storms into the kitchen to finish preparing dinner and Don turns up the volume on the TV set.

What has just occurred is unfortunate. Janet tried to be honest about her feelings and criticized Don in an attempt to get him to understand and to encourage him to change his behavior. Instead, she made things worse.

Janet ought to keep in mind the purpose of criticism. As we've noted throughout this book, criticism should be delivered in such a way that it will bring about a change in behavior. In Janet's case, criticizing Don wasn't having the desired effect.

Instead, Janet should have tried to clarify what she really wants, which is that she wants to spend more time with Don. To achieve this, Janet could have used a more creative, nonconfron-tational approach. For example, she could call Don up at work and invite him out for dinner at his favorite restaurant. Or she could arrange a dinner with friends. She could even just suggest taking a walk or sitting on the patio before dinner.

Another approach could be for Janet to simply plan a romantic evening at home. Instead of criticizing him for watching TV, she could "join him" by preparing a special dinner and serving it in the television room. She could carry on conversations with Don during the commercials, being careful not to criticize him or to bring up problems, because chances are great that Don's been dealing with them all day and is not in the mood to talk about them now. If Janet has a specific problem to discuss with him, she could apprise him of this and set aside some time to discuss it later.

Nick and Carla live down the block from Don and Janet. Nick and Carla argue because Carla never gets to go out for dinner. She likes to eat out and Nick doesn't. For the longest time, Carla has unsuccessfully tried to get him to take her out. She uses the same basic approach as Janet: she constantly complains about having to cook after working all day. As in Janet's case, if the criticism isn't bringing about the desired change in behavior, then Carla needs to try something else. Otherwise, whenever Carla starts this conversation, Nick will think to himself, "Here we go again. I already know she likes to eat out. Why does she keep harping on it?" Nick also begins to worry that if he gives in and takes her out once, she'll expect him to do it on a regular basis.

Carla could avoid directly criticizing Nick by asking friends to invite them for dinner or to meet at a restaurant. Carla could also look into joining a club where they could both enjoy scheduled dinner meetings every month or so. If none of these alternatives proves successful, she can simply arrange to go out to dinner with friends and leave Nick leftovers.

The important point to keep in mind here is that if the criticism you're delivering is not bringing about the desired change in your partner's behavior, do something else. By constantly using ineffective criticism, we become part of the problem.

In cases like Janet's and Carla's, it may be best to remain silent. Always being totally honest with your spouse can become counterproductive and can cause hurt feelings on both sides.

ACCUMULATION

A unique aspect of any relationship is the accumulation of experiences, both positive and negative. Here, let's focus on the accumulation of negative experiences—the ones that arise from mistakes. Unquestionably, family relationships tend to generate more mistakes than work relationships. In work environments, the situation changes constantly; employees get promoted or transferred, or you can learn to get on better with your boss. And, of course, at work we are expected to be polite always. But marriage builds on a long-term commitment. Because of the "accumulation phenomenon," it's easy to overreact when your spouse makes a mistake. You are not just criticizing your partner for this particular blunder, but for the accumulation of mistakes that have occurred and may yet occur.

To deal with the accumulation phenomenon, it's helpful if partners learn to view their mates as they are, not as they should be. Doing this has a twofold benefit. First, new, more constructive patterns begin to emerge. Partners begin to see each other more objectively.

Madeleine is a good example of realistic insight. She's been married to Tim for five years. She used to get extremely upset when Tim would yell at her for any mistake that she made. She even believed that his outbursts indicated that he wanted a divorce. So in desperation she would shout back questions like: "Are you going to divorce me because I accidentally erased one of your tapes?" But when Madeleine attempted to see Tim objectively, she realized that he yells and exaggerates with everyone he is upset with, not just her. Now she doesn't take his criticisms as personally as she did before.

Viewing partners more objectively also lessens our tendency to overreact. When partners begin to eliminate the "should"s and "must"s from their vocabularies, their *expectations* about each other become more realistic, stress levels diminish, and it becomes easier to assess the importance of the criticism as it relates to the bigger picture. Partners are also better able to accept one another and seek alternative ways to handle a situation. In some cases, it can mean taking direct action, as in the case of a messy house. If one partner prefers a clean, uncluttered house and the other doesn't care, it's not the end of the world and doesn't have to be a major source of daily aggravation. If the clutter becomes too irritating, the neater partner could simply take the time necessary to straighten things up or could hire someone to clean the house on a regular basis.

Tom used to get extremely upset with his wife, Brenda, because the house was always so cluttered and unkempt. His stress level would soar because he would keep thinking that the house should be clean and orderly.

Eventually, Tom came to realize that dealing with the messy house by yelling at Brenda wasn't the most effective way to handle the situation. Instead, Tom changed the way he viewed the matter. He started to think about Brenda more objectively. As soon as he did this, Tom determined that his wife was not and most likely would never be a meticulous housekeeper like his mother; besides, his mother was a full-time homemaker while Brenda held a full-time job. Tom began to see the situation as much less important than he originally imagined. Now he simply accepts that things are the way they are. If Brenda pitches in and cleans up, that's great. If she doesn't, it's not the end of the world or their relationship. To ensure that the house stays clean, Tom and Brenda agreed to hire a maid once a week.

ANGER IN INTIMATE RELATIONSHIPS

Anger doesn't destroy relationships. According to Dr. Hendrie Weisinger in his *Anger Workout Book,* not being able to work out the anger will dramatically increase the chances that a marriage will be disrupted by infidelity, physical or verbal abuse, a growing feeling of "distance," daily arguing, power struggles, and divorce. Holding back or denying anger, concurs psychiatrist David Viscott (writing in the August 1987 issue of *Woman*), can poison relationships, rob us of happy times, and insidiously destroy the joy in life. And failing to express anger can take a severe toll on our health. Psychiatrist Gerald Kushel, author of *Centering,* has found that anger that's denied can cause psychosomatic heart disease, migraine headaches, ulcers, backaches, and sexual difficulties.

The point here is not whether you should or shouldn't act angry. More importantly, it's how a couple can deal with anger when it arises. Many approaches have been suggested: expressing your feelings, writing yourself a letter about what's making you angry, taking a walk, soaking in a warm bath, slamming a door, or just taking time out.

Here are two traditional approaches that might be helpful:

1. This technique, which needs to be used only at strategic times by the nonangry partner, is credited to Dr. Murray Banks, a psychiatrist and renowned professional speaker. He recommends that when your partner is really angry, you should try humor to improve the situation. Say nothing verbally. Instead, make a funny face and gesticulate with your arms in such a way as to indicate that someone is crazy. When this approach is timed well, the angry person typically gets a shocked look and then laughs. Humor is a valuable resource, and it's one we too easily overlook. There has been little interest in researching the role of humor in

our lives, but the subject of humor and its use dates back to Aristotle.

Norman Cousins claimed that watching Marx brothers movies and other comedy films helped him to recover from a debilitating illness, and researchers have confirmed the healthy power of laughter. Most recently, Alice M. Isen, a psychologist at the University of Maryland in Baltimore, has suggested that the boost we receive from hearing a good joke is similar to the feeling we get when we receive an unexpected gift. Such elation, according to Dr. Isen, facilitates innovation. Dr. Isen's research also suggests that after hearing a joke, the mind is not so rigidly focused on negatives because we are feeling more cheerful.

2. Another idea comes from Dr. Albert Ellis, a psychologist famed for his work in rational-emotive therapy. Dr. Ellis recommends that when a person is angry with a spouse because of a mistake that the spouse has made, the receiver of the criticism can help the spouse deal effectively with the anger if something like this is said: "I realize I made a mistake and can understand why you're angry, but what are you doing to make yourself so upset?" Then pause and wait for a response. A related approach is to stop for a moment and, when the spouse has the partner's full attention, say, "Excuse me?" It's important to say this loudly, so your partner can hear you, and to phrase it as a question. Because you asked it as a question, your spouse will start repeating what was said. In the process, the angry party begins to hear the way he or she overreacted. It's also great if you can give your mate a big kiss. For, as Ingrid Bergman once said, "A kiss is a lovely trick designed by nature to stop speech when words become superfluous."

SEX AND MARRIAGE AND CRITICISM

Human beings, according to distinguished scientist Ashley Montagu, are fully equipped at birth to function as creatures who not only want and need to be loved by others, but who also want and need to love others. Probably the most intimate form of communicating love to another person is sexual intercourse. Sex transcends the physical aspects of lovemaking; it is a free expression of self, with a union of two different personalities. Lovemaking involves the mind at least as much as it involves the body.

Sex can be silly and playful. On the other hand, because it is so personal, sex can also be a way of controlling and hurting people. Men and women can withdraw sexual expectations as a way of showing disapproval. Criticizing a mate's sexual performance can have a devastating effect. In fact, criticizing your spouse during sex is never a good idea. When criticism is verbalized during sex, a person's total being is perceived as being criticized, which can shake a person's confidence badly. Rarely will it improve matters.

If you have the choice of criticizing your partner during sex or remaining silent, you're much better off remaining silent. Even though you may be honestly expressing your opinion, you also may be damaging your sexual relationship. However, this doesn't preclude you from expressing your desires and wants. Criticism is only one communication tool available for bringing about changes in someone else's behavior. Because the receiver is in control of how he or she perceives a message, criticizing your mate, even with the best intentions, is risky.

Try other forms of communication first. A golden rule of marriage that many couples subscribe to is "Whatever we want, we must do ourselves." This principle builds from the old saying "What goes around comes around." You say things that you want your mate to say to you in return.

If you feel it is necessary to use criticism during sex be sure to follow psychologist Dr. Gwendolyn Grant's advice to her clients: "Always precede the criticism with praise. This is a must, because we are bombarded with so much information about sex that people are already concerned about their sexuality and whether they are performing according to what's out there on the newsstands."

IN-LAWS

Whether in a Shakespearean play, on a vaudeville stage, or in the lyrics of songs, conflicts with in-laws never fail to strike a responsive chord with audiences. In-laws are the classic givers of criticism.

The Simmons Market Research Bureau/Bright Enterprises study on criticism revealed that criticism from in-laws was rated by research participants as the number one source of resentment!

This finding may come as no surprise, but what's interesting is that participants not only resented criticism from their in-laws but they didn't believe they needed to take action on this criticism. Instead, they rejected it out of hand, even at the risk of "paying a price."

Let's take a closer look at what's behind all the jokes that comedians have been able to cash in on for so many years and that have contributed to the stereotype popularized by the song "Mother-in-Law." The meddling in-laws are stock characters in our society, and, according to our surveys, the stereotype is something of a reality.

Perhaps the resentment that married couples feel toward their in-laws is an outgrowth of how the in-laws tend to deliver criticism—as if it were an indisputable fact. They also convey the message that a price will be paid for failing to act on their criticism. Having to deal with these attitudes leaves the couples uneasy and resentful.

There are a number of verbal and nonverbal ways in which in-laws typically express criticism. The following examples may strike you as all too familiar:

- Your mother-in-law opens your refrigerator and starts cleaning it out.
- She rearranges pots and pans in the cupboard.
- Your mother-in-law offers to change your child's bed linens.

Such nonverbal criticism can be even more subtle, as when the entire family is sitting together in the living room to watch a videotape of their daughter's recent wedding, and amid all the oohing and aahing over the bride, no one makes any mention of the new son-in-law. It's also in their tone of voice, a look on their faces, or statements like "You're happy, aren't you, dear?" and "Sweetheart, you look a little thin, are you eating enough?" And, of course, the classic "Honey, I know it's none of my business but . . ."

Criticism by in-laws can provoke special resentment when it is passed along and delivered by one of the children: for example, "Grandma said that you weren't organized and that's why you couldn't find those papers last night." Or "Grandpa said that when he was raising you, Dad, he would go out every night to play catch with you and would go to almost all your baseball games. Betcha that was great, huh, Dad?" In each of these cases, the intention is unclear and this adds to the resentment. The Simmons Market Research Bureau/Bright Enterprises survey revealed that besides taking criticism from in-laws personally, marital couples want to sort out the intention behind the criticism. Are the in-laws really trying to help, they wonder, or are they trying to interfere for destructive reasons? In-laws' criticism is usually considered to be off limits.

In-laws also tend to store up their criticisms. This is another instance of the "accumulation phenomenon" we discussed earlier. From the in-laws' perspective, of course, this accumulating is appropriate. After all, their son or daughter is involved, and they want to do what's best for him or her. It's as if they've earned the right to play the role of wise, righteous parents. When they aren't allowed to fulfill this role, they feel defeated—and someone must pay for their defeat.

Sometimes the tyranny has no end. They repeatedly "throw the stone and hide their hand," as Dr. Grant says. When you call it to their attention, they cover it with an "Oh, I'm crushed that you would think that," and as soon as things calm down, they'll plot some more.

Of course, not all in-laws are so Machiavellian. But with many in-laws whose advice on an issue hasn't been acted on to their satisfaction, there will be repercussions at some point.

All this is not to say that relationships with in-laws don't frequently bring much joy and happiness to a family's life—they do. But as many interviewees noted, serious conflicts can arise as a result of criticism. How to handle criticism with in-laws in order to break criticism patterns is no easy task. An important consideration when developing a strategy to deal with in-law criticism is to assess the frequency of your visits.

If there are infrequent visits—say, one or two weeks a year—then a cooperative approach is recommended. Go ahead and try to do what is suggested while they are visiting you. After all, once they leave, things will most often return to normal. Stress levels can be reduced greatly if you assume that their criticism is intended to be helpful. It's also admirable to communicate openly with your spouse to make sure that both of your strategies are in sync with one another when in-laws are around. Agree on your strategy and discuss how you will not become upset when criticism is directed at you or your children.

For in-laws who visit on a more regular basis, a proactive strategy is advisable. Realizing that in-law relationships are complex and multifaceted, it's difficult to come up with specific suggestions that would accommodate every situation. However, the following approaches have been successfully used by a number of families and perhaps they might be of value to you.

Often, all kinds of relationships need a fresh start—including in-law relationships. For a fresh start, try having everyone together during a warm family occasion and invite them collectively to write out all the problems that have repeatedly occurred that have led to criticism of one sort or another.

After every family member has developed his or her list, gather all the lists and put them in one pile. Next, in front of everyone, crumple each piece of paper and throw it into a nearby wastepaper basket. Burning the papers also has a dramatic effect. This technique lets everyone know that it's time to move on. Getting family members to agree and commit to making things better from this point forward will certainly create a positive momentum. The challenge from there is to get everyone to continue to do his or her part. New beginnings are not uncommon. After all, baseball and football and basketball teams get new seasons, schools and colleges start new terms, religions and cultures have their new years—so why can't relationships have new beginnings?

If confrontations with in-laws have existed for a prolonged period of time, a good way to handle the problem is to sit down with them during a neutral time and develop a written agreement of how to get along better.

Much of the discussion should focus on how to deal with criticism when it arises, besides examining ways to avoid it. To simply have a verbal discussion is not enough, because thoughts and ideas can easily be forgotten. A written agreement not only clarifies what everyone is thinking, but it also is a way to document agreements—to establish a kind of "we the family" constitution.

SINGLES

Is being single more acceptable today or are singles more sensitive about their status than ever before? The answer probably depends almost totally on the perceptions of the single individual, and such a question is beyond the scope of this book. However, let's briefly explore some of the areas where criticism arises as a result of being single.

In comparison to their grandparents, singles today have less reason to be sensitive to the remarks of others who appear to demean or criticize their marital status. This evolving change in societal attitude is evidenced with the passing effectiveness of terms such as "old maids" or "spinsters" when one is attempting to shame single women. Just as the word "bachelors" has for many generations had a connotation of dash for unmarried men, regardless of the age, single women today, instead of being "old maids," are "swinging singles" or "bachelorettes" with career objectives and lifestyles that often are envied among many married couples.

Regardless of current social attitudes, marriage as an institution is still very much in fashion. Indeed, it seems to be coming back to the popularity level it enjoyed in the fifties, when people commonly married in their late teens and early twenties. The motivations among modern day newlyweds may be rooted in logic. For reasons of economics (two incomes provide better lifestyles) or reasons related to the end of the age of sexual liberation brought about by the fear of diseases, couples are seeking monogamous relationships. It seems that as a society we have come around almost full circle from the fifties concerning the popularity of marriage and it follows that single people might feel pressure much as they did in the fifties if they stay single "too long." This pressure can easily get translated into a kind of indirect social criticism—that unspoken Greek chorus in the background faintly murmuring, "If you aren't married or at least engaged something must be wrong."

For many people not being married is a torturous source of stress and self-debasement, not to mention disappointment. All of us either have or can remember friends who seemed obsessed with a sense of insecurity until they were married. Invariably their conversations would center on the availability of eligible mates and how they seemed to be dwindling with each passing day or how the increasing proportion of gays in our society was personally affecting their dreams of wedding bells and white fences. Quite often these same people unfairly set themselves up as a target for self-criticism by putting dates on their marital objectives. They might say, for instance, "I want to be married at twenty-five—not before or after!" They unrealistically suppose that they have full control of the matter.

Such people are often very intelligent and highly achievement-oriented. As their objective date nears with the prospect of marriage unlikely, they begin to engage in self-criticism. They criticize their looks, personality, professional status, ethnicity, or a slew of other things in an attempt to help explain why their objective hasn't been met. In time, such self-criticism can have serious consequences. It can result in a debilitating loss of self-confidence, self-esteem, and on rare occasions can lead to self-destruction. And why? All because of some artificially imposed goal.

There are a number of single people who enjoy being single, and remain open to establishing a long-term relationship should the "right" person come along. Often the problem for these people is defining the meaning of "right." The tendency is to be highly critical of their prospective Mr. or Mrs. Right. One professional friend explained to me: "Many successful people believe that, because they have invested in themselves, they can't afford to step down." As a result, they tend to be critical of the "big things" as well as the "little things." There's no room for the lowering of standards. If a date—a potential partner—is not adept in social situations or doesn't have a sense of humor and self-confidence, these things get noted and get criticized accordingly—sometimes viciously.

The best advice that can be given to singles who use criticism as we've just discussed, is to keep both the "giver" and "receiver" flowcharts close at hand. As the giver, it means making sure that the "intention" behind the criticism is clearly understood. If engaging in self-criticism, be sure to refer to the receiver flowchart to check out the validity behind what's being expressed.

FRIENDS

Of course, having a good support system is invaluable in helping to handle criticism. That's where friends come in—they can be trusted, they will listen objectively and express their thoughts. At the same time, friends possess the sensitivity that's often needed—that special kind of nurturance and support that each of us desires when we really hurt inside and feel overwhelmed. Friends help to sort out the elements of the criticism that is communicated from others, as well as the kind that is self-imposed.

Defining "friendship," or what exactly it is that characterizes a friend, is far more difficult than discussing what a friend is not. If friends were viewed on a spectrum of various qualities, we might place some friends on a more cooperative scale than others. Some would be perceived as more reliable, some more interesting, others more or less sociable, fun, or argumentative. But all friends regardless of their differences would share a common quality—trustworthiness.

Among other things, time is an important factor that helps to shape that special core of friends which we describe as "good friends" or our "best friends." By the time friends become "good friends," we can usually count on very few surprises in their behavior. Words such as "reliable," "dependable," "loyal," "honest," and "fair" are some words we use to describe that special trust relationship evolving from experiences over time.

The level or degree of trust that has been nurtured and developed relates to the mutuality of faith that we have in their behavior. "She's a friend I can always rely on" . . . "You're a friend who I know will always be there when I need you" . . . "We'll be friends through thick and thin" . . . are phrases all of us have heard and have used to describe relationships which have become solidified over time.

We frequently consider our mates to be our best friends. Often, too, our parents, fellow workers and even our bosses—these are the people whom we most often rely on and for whom we have developed an interpersonal foundation of trust. These are the people whose advice we learn to most value and often whose criticism has most meaning to us.

For people whom we deeply trust are those who, more often than not, have our best interest in mind and in heart. When our best friends are not our mates or our bosses, there exists a less complex relationship not impeded by economic or obligatory unity. Such relationships can be terminated with little ado and exist because of a kind of purity of will by both parties. It is just this simplicity that often makes criticism coming from a friend the purest and most valuable. In the "just friends" relationship, much thought is given before a criticism is ever delivered so as to ensure that it is warranted and received as intended; otherwise it could fracture the relationship.

This is not to say that we should trust what our friends say more than our mates or bosses when it comes to criticism, but chances are a friend has little to gain by criticizing us.

The Simmons/Bright criticism research study showed that only 8 percent of respondents either strongly resent or resent criticism from a friend while 22 percent resent criticism from their spouse. These statistics could be indicative of the fact that when friends give criticism it is perceived more as advice that doesn't require action or remediation, while when spouses give criticism, action and remediation are expected—action or remediation that we might "resent" having to take.

CHILDREN

"I can't believe this," said Sara during our interview. "I never really paid attention to how I criticized my kids. I just did it. If Melissa came into the room and asked me what I thought of her blouse, "I'd just tell her that I liked the pink one better. I never thought to explain to her *why* I felt the pink blouse would look more attractive. I wonder if she ever really learned from situations when I criticized her."

Debbie echoes this sentiment even more poignantly. Last year, she lost a son in a tractor accident and she says regretfully, "If I had to do it over again, I never would criticize my son as much as I did. The things I criticized him about were so trivial. I would yell at him for leaving his shirttail out with the same intensity as I would for not finishing a report for school on time. It would have been better if I had distinguished different degrees of importance."

At home, many families seem to dole out criticism as if, like James Bond, they have a "license to kill." They feel they have free rein to criticize as often as they want because they believe it to be for "everyone's own good."

Parents in general do not pay close enough attention to how they criticize their children, nor are they given to pondering the consequences of their criticism. This is a mistake, because children are quite different from adults.

Dr. Tessa Warschaw, psychologist and author of several best-selling books, points out that children have a narrower experience base than adults. This fact produces several interesting side effects. First, children don't know about logical consequences, whereas adults do; parents are constantly reminding them to think before they do something.

Furthermore, children have unsophisticated judgment. They tend to view the consequences of their actions solely in terms of leading to either reward or punishment. For example, if an adult repeatedly performs poorly on the job, that adult knows that he or she might get fired. If a child, on the other hand, does poorly, all the child knows is that he or she will get punished. If nothing happens, the child will interpret the lack of punishment as a reward.

Furthermore, children are not as well equipped to handle criticism as are adults. They aren't aware of a wide range of options. When children are criticized, they can do one of two things. First, they can try to please the adult in an attempt to gain his or her love, or they can defy the adult and cause a lot of turmoil.

As a result, criticizing a child without giving that child an opportunity to learn, to change an undesirable behavior, or to discuss the issue has more lasting consequences than with adults. The criticism hits deeper and lasts longer because children don't have as much experience to draw upon. Like adults, children can implement only what they understand and what they are capable of doing.

When parents criticize a child because "it's for his or her own good," they often instill a misguided sense of self-esteem. They tell their child, "If you *do* this right or if you *act* right, then you are a good person." For example, a mother who tells her son, "Don't spill the milk," will say "*Good boy*" if he doesn't. Children thus learn that to be accepted they have to act properly, instead of learning that they will be loved regardless of how they act. This is why so many of us—children and adults alike—yearn desperately for unconditional love.

Parents need to be careful, because 99 out of 100 times, children will see themselves as rotten when they are criticized. Dr. Albert Ellis explained to me that when a child has done something wrong, a rational reaction might be: "I've done something wrong and next time I'll do better." But the average child's response is more likely irrational: "I did the wrong thing. I'm no good." And while a more rational person might react to doing the wrong thing with temporary regret or disappointment, the child, because he or she tends to overgeneralize, may suffer a lasting loss of self-esteem. If this type of criticism persists, the child may do what you ask, but he or she will not be happy.

The consequences of criticizing a child severely can be devastating, over both the short and the long term. Ellen, age fifty-three, is a good example. Ellen's mother was very critical, so as a girl she would always go to her father because he was more supportive. "It's funny," she notes. "The things I feel good about now were the things my father used to praise me for. The areas where I'm not confident, my father said nothing." Ellen confided to me that her mother *never* told her she was pretty, even on her wedding day. To this day, she doesn't think of herself as attractive.

Then there's Richard, who was always critical of his only son, Ken. Ever since Ken was a little boy, Richard would tell him that he would never amount to anything. "Well, at age thirty-six," Anne, the young man's mother comments bitterly, "the kid is nothing—just like his father said he would be." Being careless about the way criticism is communicated to children can destroy their confidence and the way they see themselves. As we've noted earlier, we must all beware of contributing to self-fulfilling prophecies.

The question is not *whether* parents need to criticize their kids, but *how*. Experts suggest that because children are vulnerable, we need to point out that what they *did* was wrong without letting them feel that they are terrible people. For example, if your child spills milk, Dr. Albert Ellis recommends that you say, "You spilled the milk. It would be better if you didn't, but we all make mistakes. After all, you *only* spilled the milk." Similarly, if your child comes home with a report card filled with C's and D's, you should say something like, "You'll have to work harder next term because grades are very important. But, on the other hand, grades aren't *everything* and I still love you very much."

This brings us to another essential communication skill to keep in mind when dealing with children. Children need to be taught the logical consequences of their actions. Dr. Tessa Warschaw emphasizes that it's essential for parents to talk to their children in terms of logical consequences. For instance, you should tell your son, "Johnny, you must rake the leaves by Friday. If you don't, I'll assume you were too busy and you will do it on Saturday, instead of going to the movies with your friends." If bedtime on Friday comes along and the leaves haven't been raked, the parent can then say, "I guess you didn't want to go badly enough, so I'll see you around the house tomorrow."

Dealing with your child in this way resembles the management of expectations among adults (see chapter 6). However, the child is receiving training in the consequences of his or her actions. An advantage to this strategy is that the punishment component is minimized. The child also learns to take responsibility for his or her actions. Finally, the child has a greater opportunity to do what is expected of him or her.

This approach benefits the parents as well: it helps to minimize their need to criticize, and it frees them from having to wear their police officer's uniform all the time.

But what if the child rebels and yells back at the parent? In this case, the parents need to maintain their perspective and not globalize the issue by thinking, "That's just the way kids are." Parents should refer to the receiver's flowchart (see page 29). The child is simply communicating information. The receiver, or parent, has the control over how to perceive the information— whether to accept or reject it, or whether to take action or ignore it. When the flowchart is used as it is intended, the parent is not only acknowledging that the criticism is important, but he or she is better able to consider the *validity* of the criticism objectively, without taking it personally.

You can deal with a rebellious outburst by telling your child coolly, "Well, you may be right, you know, but why are you so upset that I'm wrong? After all, everyone is wrong sometimes." This technique is effective because the parent overtly acknowledges and evaluates the child's criticism, and the child is encouraged to reflect on how he or she is reacting. The child therefore is able to move from "I hate everything! Everything is horrible!" to "I'm upset and disappointed about this specific issue."

Another way to handle a child's outburst is to do what my friend Gwen did. Her teenage daughter was extremely upset over something that Gwen did. She started screaming at Gwen at the top of her lungs, "I hate you, I hate you." Gwen stood by calmly until her daughter appeared to have finished her invective. Gwen said, "I know you do, dear. I hated my mother at times, too." At that moment, her daughter was shocked and speechless. Before she could open her mouth, Gwen put her arms around her and gave her a long hug. Her daughter clung to her mother with tears streaming down her eyes. Gwen confessed that she uses this approach only rarely. "I guess I learned it from my mom," she admits. "She was so accepting of me and my moods. She was such a secure woman."

Sometimes, if parents observe their child carefully, they will notice that certain patterns emerge. For example, they may discover that the child is setting himself or herself up for criticism in an effort to attract attention. In addition, looking for patterns gives a parent an opportunity to decide whether criticism is the best approach to use to direct a child's behavior.

For instance, Fern and Paul know that every time they take their six-year-old son swimming, he never wants to get out of the water. Each time, a hassle ensues and the boy leaves the pool with wet eyes and a sullen expression. If the parents had remembered this usual outcome before going swimming, this scene could probably have been avoided, but let's say they forgot: they now need to do something different.

Invent a game. We all like to play games. In this game, the first one out of the pool gets the biggest towel. After a while, the reward may become superfluous; the fun derives from playing the game. From years of personal experience, I can assure you that if there's enthusiasm in your voice, the child will respond.

Another creative approach worked well for Susan and her ten-year-old son, Sammy. Every day, Sammy came home from school with a gloomy look on his face and brought up only negative things about his day. Susan kept telling him to stop being so negative, but this didn't help.

I suggested that Susan try the following: instead of criticizing her son for being so negative, invent a game that both Sammy and his eight-year-old sister, Tammy, can play. Each day when they come home from school, each child gets to play the first part of the game—five minutes of negative discussion. In other words, whatever is said for five minutes has to be negative. When the five minutes are up, part two of the game begins. Part two lasts until dinnertime. During these next three hours, *everyone*, including Mom, needs to say only positive things. If anyone says something negative, then the other family members chime in and remind him or her that it's "Positive Time." For Susan, this worked extraordinarily well. Everybody had a grand time. If Dad happened to come home early, he got to play the game, too. As a result, Sammy dropped all his negative talk easily after the first five minutes. "Now our only challenge," Susan wrote to me, "is that we are trying to come up with a name for the game—any suggestions?"

Chapter 8

CRITIHOLICS

You're invited to a party! There'll be plenty of food, the bar will be well stocked—and the conversation is sure to be provocative. You see, all of the guests have something special in common. We'll call them "critiholics"—people who, either consciously or unconsciously, thrive on receiving criticism and actually invite it from almost everyone they encounter: friends, lovers, bosses, clients, fellow employees, even store clerks.

Despite their best intentions, critiholics repeatedly act out their own self-destructive tendencies. They may not be aware (or they do a good job of denying the truth) that they set themselves up to be criticized, and having received the criticisms they invoke, they can respond only by focusing on their hurt feelings. The underlying value of the criticism is never recognized, and the cycle begins anew.

The party began a half hour ago, so gather up your courage, ring the doorbell, greet your hostess, and meet the other guests. You're in for a memorable evening!

Critiholic #1: The "Poor Organizer"

Carrie is our hostess, and she greets us with a friendly smile. "I'm so glad you could come!" she exclaims. We smile back at her, but we can't help noticing her wrinkled skirt and her coffee-stained blouse. "All my good dresses are at the cleaner's." She shrugs indifferently. "I forgot to take them in until this morning, and they weren't ready on my way home tonight."

Carrie's guests look at each other and wink knowingly. For years, she's been satisfied with mediocrity and never makes adequate preparation. Perhaps worst of all, she doesn't even try to anticipate potential areas of conflict from which criticism could arise.

For example, four of tonight's guests are vegetarians. However, all of the hors d'oeuvres contain meat. A number of the guests smoke, and still another group are staunch nonsmokers. But a blue haze pervades among the chitchat. No one wants a confrontation, so resentment is simmering under the surface, and it's directed at Carrie for not having taken these matters into consideration. One simple solution would have been to designate one room as a "smoker," but Carrie just didn't think of it. "I don't know why I bother to come to Carrie's parties," one guest confides to another, "she always botches things." "Yes," the second guest replies, "but it's kind of fun to guess in advance what will happen next. At the same time, it's unfortunate she never changes, even though her friends try to help her become more organized."

Critiholic #2: The "Agreement Breaker"

A couple of women at the party are really annoyed that Carrie has invited Roger. In fact, they're surprised he even bothered to show up. After all, he had once asked each of them out for a date, but each time he failed to appear at the appointed time and place.

Now Roger is wondering why these women are giving him the cold shoulder.

Breaking agreements is a way of life with Roger. Not only does he break social engagements, he's in trouble with his boss for missing an important deadline on a key project. "So what if it's a day or two late?" he appeals to Isabel, another guest whom we are about to meet. "We're too concerned about time in Western culture. You know, in the Middle East, if you make a date for noon, no one expects you to show up until three. Now that's the kind of life I admire. Don't you agree?"

Critiholic #3: The "Go-getter"

Isabel doesn't have much tolerance for Roger's dawdling and laid-back attitude. She's always on the move: the fast-track type who never takes time to slow down and assess who she really is or what her goals are in life. She associates periodic stasis with laziness and nonproductivity, instead of seeing "down time" as essential for self-regeneration.

How does she consistently invite criticism? By taking on challenges that are so removed from her area of expertise that those with whom she interacts roll their eyes and say, "Oh, not *this* again."

For example, just three weeks ago, Isabel read a current best seller on coping with stress. She is so excited about her newfound area of knowledge that she has decided to market herself as an expert in the field. She's already pulled together an outline for a two-day seminar and is exploring different types of advertising to attract participants. But Isabel has given no thought to her overall commitment to this new project. After all, she works full-time as a department-store display director. Where does her stress workshop fit into her professional life? Is it ethical to promote herself as a stress expert when she's clearly a novice? Does the world really need yet another "self-help" seminar? So, once again, Isabel's friends shake their heads when she announces her latest scheme.

Critiholic #4: The "Opinion Seeker"

Tim lacks self-confidence. Nobody's come over to talk to him, so he's standing alone in a corner of the living room holding a plate of hors d'oeuvres.

When Tim does talk to people, he usually asks them for advice. For years, it seems, he has been waiting to move to a new apartment, but he's been daunted by the wide range of alternatives. Should he buy or rent? Should he find a better apartment in his present neighborhood or move to an area closer to his office? And so on. Everyone he speaks to seems to have a different opinion about what he should do, but they've all agreed about one thing: Tim is a wimp. "You'll *never* leave that apartment," Ingrid snapped at him earlier this evening. "Why, you can't even decide on your own about where you want to eat dinner or what movie you want to see. It's always, 'I don't know! What do *you* want to do?' " Although Ingrid is certainly not the most popular person at the party, all the guests share her frustration with Tim.

Critiholic #5: The "Quick Draw" Criticizer

Have you ever met a person who is always quick to criticize? If you haven't, meet Ingrid. She always has her finger on the criticism trigger. Anyone who passes by her sights is subject to a blast of criticism. She goes out of the way to make sure she gets her criticism licks in first.

You can recognize Ingrid with one quick glance: she's the woman complaining bitterly about the cigarette smoke blowing in her face! Already preparing her critical attack on Carrie, her hostess, Ingrid, it seems clear, walks into every situation ready to find fault.

Always quick to criticize everything around her, Ingrid marches into all encounters expecting the worst. A casual shopping excursion may well turn into a brouhaha. She may criticize the way her companions dress or wear makeup; or she may claim loudly that the prices are too high, the quality of the merchandise is inferior, and the salespeople are rude and unhelpful.

Last week, Ingrid was in her glory when she set out to return an electronic typewriter she had just bought. In her mind, she had already imagined her upcoming argument with the sales clerk. Ingrid presented the typewriter to the clerk, who politely queried, "What's the problem with it? Are you sure you read the directions correctly?" Ingrid retorted, "I *knew* this was going to happen! I won't put up with your belligerent attitude! Get me the manager!" Consistently anticipating confrontation and harsh words in her exchange with others, Ingrid is rarely off guard and always ready for a verbal duel.

The main disadvantage of her quick-draw tactic is that it comes back to haunt her . . . in the form of criticism.

Critiholic #6: The "Ostrich"

Like an ostrich that buries its head in the sand, Harry often fails to recognize the realities of certain situations. As a result, he invites criticism from those around him who are more perceptive. His "blind side" often causes him to misread the unspoken messages, and this tends to leave him open to criticism, especially on the job.

At an office party last week, for example, Harry danced again and again with his boss's attractive wife. While it was apparent to most of those present that the boss had taken notice and was not pleased by Harry's behavior, Harry blithely continued his dance-floor antics. Somehow, the other employees knew that their boss is the jealous type—but not Harry, and, as on previous occasions, his refusal to recognize what was going on would be his downfall. In a staff meeting the following Monday, the boss called all his department heads together to discuss their performances. Pointing to Harry and referring to him as "Fred Astaire," he said, "A couple of your people always come in late—why don't you do something about it?" And "You came in way over budget on that video project. Why can't you keep track of your expenses?" Baffled, Harry later asked his associates what he had done to deserve such criticism. And why did the boss call him "Fred Astaire"?

On another memorable occasion, Harry was responsible for making a presentation to a client whom we'll refer to as "Bull Dog," a stocky, feisty man who used his loud, angry voice to intimidate others. Everyone else in Harry's firm acknowledged that the guy was offensive and stubborn, but since he *was* a client, they tried to overlook his abuse. Not Harry.

During the presentation, Bull Dog made his usual combative remarks: "*How* long did you say it took you to prepare this report? It's incomplete! It's worthless!" Harry's colleagues just sat back and shut up; but Harry took offense at Bull Dog's statements and fought back. It was obvious to everyone who would be the loser in the ensuing debate. But, once again, Harry failed to pick up on it. He descended to Bull Dog's level, lost the account, and gave his boss yet another opportunity to criticize him.

Critiholics #7 and #8: The "Reassurance Seekers"

Olivia and Lydia are sisters. Both are reassurance seekers, but in subtly different ways. Olivia is telling Ivan (whom we'll meet soon) about the wonderful weekend place she's sharing at the beach. "The only problem," she confesses, "is that I've lost my tan. I mean, my skin got too dry from all that sun, so I've been staying indoors a lot. I've spent a ton of money on moisturizers, but I'm still getting all these wrinkles. I've tried using vitamin E, but that hasn't made much of a difference either. Nothing seems to work."

As she's talking, Olivia is laughing, because she doesn't want Ivan to think she's really concerned about this problem. At this point, he takes a good hard look at her and concludes, "Yeah, you're right; your skin *does* look dry and your forehead is peeling. Maybe you should see a dermatologist." Suddenly incensed, Olivia haughtily tosses back her head and frostily comments, "Well, I *see.* Thank you for that wonderful piece of advice." She marches off, thinking to herself, "How dare that man criticize me like that!"

While Olivia was talking with Ivan, her sister had been chatting with Carrie, whom she hadn't seen for almost three years. They'd been laughing away as they tried to compress those years into twenty minutes of conversation. Inevitably, the topic turns to diets and weight loss. Lydia asks Carrie, "What do you think? Am I too fat? Tell me the truth; I can take it. I'd be honest with you."

Carrie looks at Lydia with frank appraisal and responds, "Well, yeah, Lydia, you could stand to firm up a little. I'd take off eight pounds, maybe twelve. . . . It's not a lot of weight to lose, you know."

That's as far as poor Carrie gets, because Lydia, angry and embarrassed, bursts out, "How can you say I need to lose eight pounds, Carrie? Just yesterday, when I got on the scale, I was only two pounds over my normal weight." Carrie quickly realizes that she's said the wrong thing and looks for a way out. She fortunately notices Ingrid—the "quick draw" criticizer—staring venomously at an empty bowl. And she blushingly stammers, "I'd better put out some more pretzels."

How do Olivia and Lydia invite criticism? Basically, by coming right out and *asking* for it. They bring up their vulnerable points and then are surprised and hurt when they get what they've asked for. The difference between them is that Olivia is comfortable with criticizing herself and she wants others to disagree, while Lydia asks people directly whether she has a problem, and expects them to say, "Oh, no, Lydia, of course not!" Both criticism seekers must learn that if they solicit an honest opinion, they should be prepared to receive one.

Critiholic #9: The "Social Norm Violator"

Ivan's a man who stands out in a crowd. Tonight, for example, he's wearing a bright red silk shirt, gaudy gold chains, and cowboy boots with three-inch heels. When you look at Ivan, you can't help but wonder what he sees when he looks in the mirror.

Ivan works for an advertising agency. Recently, he had lunch with some Pepsico executives to discuss a possible new campaign. When the waiter asked what everyone wanted to drink, Ivan ordered a Diet Coke. Later, he was surprised when the Pepsi people seemed strangely cool to his creative suggestions.

Some people may admire Ivan's highly individualistic, iconoclastic behavior; other people find it extremely irksome. Thus Ivan is faced with a choice: he can continue being his "own man," despite the consequences (such as frequently insulting the very people he needs to win over to his side, like the Pepsi executives); or he can reexamine his approach to determine how he can avoid the criticism being leveled at him.

And here he goes again! Carrie's introducing him to two women he's never met before, and he kisses each one on the cheek. One finds his approach offensive; the other thinks he's kind of gallant. One thing's for sure: Ivan will always generate controversy—and criticism—wherever he goes.

Critiholic #10: The "Fuzzy Trapper"

Clyde is full of surprises—and not always welcome ones. He once asked Isabel, the "go-getter," out on a date. "What did you have in mind?" she asked. "Something you'll enjoy," he answered with characteristic vagueness. Isabel, who, as we've seen, is an active type, quickly assumed she was in for an exciting evening at a disco. Imagine her chagrin when Clyde arrived at her apartment and announced that he'd been able to get tickets to a four-hour film about political strife in medieval Bulgaria. Isabel squirmed in her seat all evening, totally bored. When the movie was over, Isabel told him a thing or two about his ideas of what she enjoys. The problem here is that Clyde failed to clarify his expectations. He does the same thing at work. Just yesterday, he asked his assistant, Michael, to go out and get him a sandwich. "It doesn't matter what kind," he added. When Michael showed up with a ham and swiss on rye, Clyde hit the roof. "Did you have to bring me ham? I had a ham sandwich for lunch yesterday, and my girlfriend baked ham for dinner last night."

"Well, don't get upset with me," Michael retorted. "Why didn't you say so in the first place?"

Failing to clarify one's expectations is one of the easiest ways to invite criticism. In fact, many people interviewed believe that much of the criticism in the workplace can be traced to expectations that are either not expressed at all or not made sufficiently clear. So don't be a victim of criticism by getting caught in the "fuzzy trap."

SURE WAYS TO INVITE CRITICISM

Now that you've met the majority of the guests at the critiholic party, you probably are able to recognize similar critiholic tendencies in your friends, loved ones, and perhaps even in yourself.

What sets critiholics apart from other people is their habitual tendency to set themselves up for criticism. As the party-givers have demonstrated, this can be done in several ways. Let's briefly recap them:

- Being unprepared or poorly organized (Carrie)
- Breaking agreements (Roger)
- Being unaware of one's strengths and weaknesses (Isabel)
- Constantly seeking advice from others (Tim)
- Expecting a confrontation to ensue (Ingrid)
- Being blind to the realities of a situation (Harry)
- Disclosing your vulnerabilities to others (Olivia and Lydia)
- Disregarding social norms (Ivan)
- Failing to clarify expectations (Clyde)

As we've seen in earlier chapters, criticism is an inevitable fact of life, and we can use it as a valuable communication tool to help us clarify our wants and goals and determine how best to achieve them. However, there's no need for anyone to *invite* criticism unnecessarily into his or her life; there's enough of it circulating around as it is.

It's important to understand that critiholics reenact the same scenes of fault-finding or opinion-seeking over and over, until these personality quirks become deeply ingrained patterns. Once this occurs, the individual resorts to critiholic behavior reflexively.

Critiholics rarely think about the criticism leveled at them from others. Consequently, they tend to repeat their undesirable behaviors with marked frequency. Some critiholics simply do not understand what it is about their mannerisms that alienates others. Others distrust—and therefore dismiss—their critics, since critiholics tend not to maintain a healthy balance between emotions and rational analysis.

Because of the critiholics' tendency to focus on their own hurt feelings rather than on the information contained in the criticism, they seldom comprehend the potentially constructive power of criticism—that it helps to bring about a change of behavior that can lead to positive end results.

Let us return to the partygoers and analyze their critiholic behavior further.

They all have one thing in common: they aren't learning from the criticism they repeatedly invite.

The goal here is not to become totally insulated from criticism, but to use it effectively when it inevitably comes. What we have to do is stop repeating our vulnerability to criticism and think of it as, perhaps, a way to learn and become better at what we do and how we do it.

Chapter 9

THE ART OF
CRITICIZING
OURSELVES

As children, one of the first defenses with which we learned to arm ourselves against harsh insults from peers was the expression "Sticks and stones will break my bones, but names will never hurt me." Eleanor Roosevelt, as we pointed out earlier, conveniently rephrased this concept for us as adults when she said, "No one can make you feel inferior without your consent."

Few of us, however, have ever been given such good advice on how to mount a defense against malicious and often debilitating onslaughts from a person who is closer and more familiar to us than anyone else—our own selves.

When we criticize ourselves, we are engaging in an internal dialogue that pits us as the giver against us as the receiver. This is a very special kind of criticism interaction. There is no game-playing here. No room for such deliberations as whether the giver is "off limits" or is in a justifiable position to criticize. The criticism can't be rejected if the timing is inappropriate. All it takes to set off self-criticism is a slight misjudgment, as during a golf swing, or a miscommunication with another person.

Self-criticism is the most difficult form of criticism and unquestionably the most popular. Results from our nationwide survey revealed that more than 76 percent of the respondents identified themselves as being hard or extremely hard on themselves. What's toughest about self-criticism is that we are accountable only to ourselves if we decide not to take appropriate action. Yet, taking the appropriate action may require that we divulge our shortcomings to others, whether in the form of an apology or an admission that we failed to meet others' expectations.

What's not easy to understand is why some people, when they engage in self-criticism, are able to succeed in taking the proper corrective action, while others become immobilized or do permanent damage to their self-esteem.

WHAT IS SELF-CRITICISM?

To better understand the dynamics of self-criticism, we should first take a closer look at why and how it differs from self-evaluation. *Self-evaluation* is the process of objectively examining one's behavior and motives to determine their value in relationship to a desired end result. *Self-criticism* may be part of this process, but it involves strictly a focus on the negative aspects of behavior. It departs from self-evaluation in that it portends action. So, self-criticism is that part of the self-evaluation process that prompts action of a remedial nature.

This key feature of self-criticism can make it either a positive or a negative force in our lives. It can be good because it provides us with an opportunity to further enhance our performance and our self-confidence.

Developing good self-evaluative skills is important to our success in just about everything we do. Within the framework of developing these skills, it is mandatory that we practice a healthy attitude regarding self-criticism. Such an attitude is held by Suzanne Jaffe, president of a successful Wall Street investment banking firm: "I regard self-criticism as a valuable way to learn. You're able to assess what needs to be done better. You're able to discover where you can improve—and that in itself is motivating."

The ability to self-evaluate *accurately* and to take appropriate action has the tangential rewards of enabling us to stay in control while strengthening self-confidence. It also helps to keep us from getting caught up in our lies about ourselves. When we corrupt the process of self-evaluation, we may begin to believe in our own lies, and we eventually lose the ability to judge the credibility of praise or criticism from others. Quality self-criticism, therefore, gives us a yardstick with which we can compare criticism (and praise) received from others. It keeps us from being easily influenced by what others say about us. But self-criticism can also be devastating. A friend once confessed, "I told myself so often that I was stupid that I couldn't do anything that I really believed in. My whole life, both on the job and off, began to suffer."

Where do you fall on the spectrum of self-criticism? Do you use self-criticism to inspire yourself to new heights, or do you use it to drive yourself to new depths?

The self-criticism test that follows will help you to answer these questions.

THE SELF-CRITICISM TEST

Take a moment to answer these questions.
Be honest with your answers.

	Almost never (add 1 point)	Occasionally (add 2 points)	Frequently (add 3 points)	Almost all the time (add 4 points)
1. After you've criticized yourself do you take appropriate action?	_____	_____	_____	_____
2. After criticizing yourself, do you feel stronger and more confident?	_____	_____	_____	_____
3. Do you let go of self-criticism easily?	_____	_____	_____	_____
4. Do you avoid criticizing yourself when you are about to enter into an important activity?	_____	_____	_____	_____

	Almost never (add 1 point)	Occasionally (add 2 points)	Frequently (add 3 points)	Almost all the time (add 4 points)
5. Do you assess the validity of the self-criticism?	_____	_____	_____	_____
6. When you make a mistake, do you keep in mind the fact that you are not perfect?	_____	_____	_____	_____
7. Do you usually learn from your mistakes and as a result only have to criticize yourself one time for your actions?	_____	_____	_____	_____
8. Do you practice making sure that your self-criticisms are specific?	_____	_____	_____	_____
9. Are you aware of when you are criticizing yourself?	_____	_____	_____	_____
10. Are you able to let go of the negative effects of self-criticism when you are in the act of performing a task (for example, tennis match, public speaking)?	_____	_____	_____	_____
11. Are you good at not berating yourself mentally after you've made a serious mistake?	_____	_____	_____	_____
12. Do you easily fall asleep at night?	_____	_____	_____	_____
13. Do you easily keep your mistakes in proper perspective?	_____	_____	_____	_____
14. Can you laugh at your mistakes?	_____	_____	_____	_____
TOTALS	_____	_____	_____	_____

Total your score by adding the value of the columns checked.

Score		Interpretation
50–56	_____	You're learned how to use self-criticism as an effective tool for enhancing your performance and your self-confidence.
43–49	_____	You're pretty good at working with yourself. Depending on your mood, you may need to work a little harder at keeping self-criticism in a productive, useful light.
36–42	_____	Average. You're bordering on being hard on yourself.
31–35	_____	You're probably too tough on yourself. This could be simply because you never learned how to use self-criticism constructively.
26–30	_____	There's probably no need for others to criticize you. You're saying, "You don't have to criticize me, I'm tough enough on myself."
Below 25	_____	You're an expert! You're extremely good at making yourself miserable and probably talk yourself out of getting involved in a lot of different activities. You've done a good job at using self-criticism to shatter your confidence. Just think of your potential: if you're so good at using self-criticism for destructive purposes, think what you could do if you learned to use it productively.

HOW TO DEAL WITH SELF-CRITICISM

Now that you have a better idea where you stand with regard to self-criticism, let's explore what you can do to handle it better.

Keep in mind that you can't eliminate or avoid self-criticism. It's a natural activity—and an important one, as we've discussed. However, it needs to be channeled and managed properly. A person who has learned to do this will typically say, "I'm good to myself" or "I've learned to work with myself."

The key word here is "learned," because, like any skill, constructive self-criticism must be learned.

Start by Listening to Yourself

Most of us are aware of our own self-talk, especially when we engage in self-criticism. However, some of us get so accustomed to our self-talk that we may just let the words fly by unnoticed.

For example, Terry sells machine-type fasteners on the West Coast. After he calls on a client and gets back into his car to organize his papers and make notes of certain key points the client made, he will silently call himself stupid and accuse himself of being incompetent. If the client decided not to take advantage of his services, Terry is quick to blame himself and dismiss the possibility that perhaps the client was simply not interested in the fasteners he sells. All of this mental self-abuse would take place without Terry's full awareness. He likened it to listening to the television set when you are in another room. You know the TV is on, but you're not paying much attention to what is being said.

But it's as important to listen to what we are saying to ourselves as it is to listen when our partner or boss is criticizing us. As soon as Terry started to pay attention and listen to his own inner conversations, he was appalled. He was reminded of something he'd been asked years earlier: "If you had a friend who talked to you the way you talk to yourself, would you still have him or her as your friend?" Terry, without a second thought, said "NO!"

When you really listen, not only will you discover new information about yourself but you also will begin to interpret negatives in a nonjudgmental way. Terry, for instance, was told simply to interpret the information as "Isn't this interesting," rather than getting down on himself for becoming aware of how frequently he has engaged in destructive self-criticism. When listening to your inner talk, pretend you're eavesdropping on a conversation between two strangers and listen without being judgmental.

Taking the time to listen to ourselves is a worthwhile investment because the words we use are very powerful, and our self-talk provides us with invaluable information that we need to sort out.

Words produce reactions within us that may be physical, emotional, chemical, hormonal, or mental. To prove this point, take a moment to close your eyes and imagine yourself taking a big juicy orange (*pause*), slicing it open (*pause*), and then taking a bite. If you do this exercise, you'll notice that your mouth starts to salivate in anticipation of eating the juicy orange. Many of us would also have envisioned picking up the orange and putting it on a counter or a cutting board. Besides reacting physiologically, we are able to visualize the orange, feel the orange as we touch it, hear the knife cut through it, and perhaps even smell and taste it as well. All of our senses are activated, just by using words.

As another example of the tremendous impact that words can have, consider the times you've said to yourself, "I'm so tired." After saying this, have you ever felt more lethargic? If imagining a minor pleasure like eating an orange can trigger our senses so strongly, then can you imagine the tremendous impact that calling ourselves "stupid" has, especially if we discover that we do this countless times a day?

As Jay, a project manager for one of the largest U.S. banks, said, "We talk ourselves into it." Jay used to constantly berate himself for procrastinating. He would call himself lazy and a no-good bum. At times, he would even tell himself that he'd never get anywhere in his career if he kept procrastinating. Besides convincing himself of this during his own self-talk, he reinforced it further by telling others the same thing. At lunches and at other social gatherings, Jay would bring up the fact that one of his biggest and most troublesome problems was procrastination.

Just think of the time and energy Jay invested in persuading himself that he is a procrastinator—time better spent doing that which he was putting off!

Look for Patterns

Instead of criticizing ourselves for the fact that we do criticize ourselves, let's explore what we criticize ourselves for. To determine this, we must look for patterns. Becoming aware of patterns better enables us to recognize our behavior and simultaneously gives us insights into how we will most likely behave in the future. For instance, many people use self-criticism to spur themselves into action. Even Jay, whether or not he was aware of it, used procrastination as a way to get things done. He could have learned this strategy in junior high school. Suppose he put off studying for an exam until the night before the test, when he burned the midnight oil. Jay took his test the next day and scored an A. From that point on, Jay may have unwittingly relied on procrastination as a motivational signal for action. Today, Jay still puts things off! While he's procrastinating, he will undergo numerous yelling matches with himself for not getting the work done until he finally reaches a point that signals him into action. This approach worked very well for Jay for a number of years. Now it's not as effective. Not only is the wear and tear on his body greater now that he's older, but he has additional responsibilities as well. If numerous projects come at him simultaneously, the pressure becomes too intense.

For many of us, like Jay, self-criticism is an inner voice that goads us into action. We also use it to help us improve ourselves. Just as praising ourselves helps to propel us to higher levels of achievement, so does self-criticism. When I interviewed Suzanne Jaffe, the New York financial investor, who has an extremely healthy attitude about self-criticism, she said, "When you criticize yourself, you're finding out ways you can improve, and that's exciting. No one has to know about your private conversations and the actions you intend to take. I think I'm hard on myself only because I believe it will make me better. It's really an analysis of what I've done and the reasons why I did it, so that I can figure out how I can do better the next time. Self-criticism means self-analysis; I'm giving myself an opportunity to bat back and forth the motives behind my actions. It helps me to put closure on situations by bringing them out in the open and studying them. Otherwise, you end up internalizing it and layer upon layer builds up. You keep thinking it will go away, but it doesn't."

Others of us, when we examine ourselves, may find that we tend to use self-criticism to knock ourselves down until we reach the point of not taking any action. If we do take action under these circumstances, we do so more by simply going through the motions, rather than by involving ourselves heart and soul.

Rob illustrates this phenomenon. He is a pitcher for one of the minor league baseball teams. He criticizes himself to such an extent prior to a game that his performance suffers. His coach can't understand it. In practice sessions he does fine, but in a game situation he falls apart. Rob discovered that his pattern was to be unusually hard on himself the night before a game. He would criticize himself for all the things he did wrong during practice sessions and focus on those errors. In addition, he would recall all his mistakes in the last game. As a result of these inner conversations, he would feel less confident about himself. He would be racked by self-doubt and uncertainty. Half of him would say, "I don't think I'll do very well today. I haven't practiced hard enough," while the other half would snap back, "How can you talk to yourself like that, you stupid idiot? You'll never win a game with an attitude like that." Rob was destined to do poorly before he ever stepped out on the field because of his own thoughts. He had defeated himself by focusing on the criticism rather than the remedy.

Brian is another case in point. He is a financial services adviser for a major New York–based financial services company. Self-criticism debilitates him and keeps him from asking for a sale. He's been in the field three years, and to this day, he will meet with a client and show all the many ways he can be of service and then not follow through by asking for the business. Brian says that before he sees the client, he uses self-criticism as a way to cause him to doubt himself. If he asks for the business and the client says no, then it only reaffirms all the things he's said to himself. It's not uncommon for Brian to continue criticizing himself even when he's talking to the client. Inwardly, he's telling himself, for example, "You're sitting the wrong way. . . . That was the wrong thing to say. . . . How could you have asked such a silly question? . . . You blew it; you'll never get the sale now. . . . She can tell you're nervous," and so on. Poor Brian—I think we all can relate to him at one time or another.

Other interviewees pointed out that they use self-criticism as a means of keeping themselves in line so they don't come across as too arrogant. Their pattern of self-talk centers on telling themselves, "Don't get too cocky. You know what happens when you think you're too good—someone will come along and knock you down. Don't think you're too good; they are just waiting to catch you." Or "You're not such hot stuff. Just remember you put your pants on one leg at a time just like everyone else." Such familiar phrases have probably been in the family many years and are instilled into each new generation. As adults, we simply have taken on the same behavior and applied it to ourselves through self-criticism.

Most of us probably are a combination of each of these patterns, with one pattern being more dominant than the others. Some of us may be unsure of the patterns we use to criticize ourselves. To gain some insight here, it's helpful to ask, "How is this helping me?" Asking yourself that question throughout a week will help provide some valuable clues.

Recognizing when we typically criticize ourselves is also valuable. For instance, there's a tendency to be more self-critical when we are tired.

Marilyn, an interviewee in the study, said, "I'm really hard on myself when I'm tired. Since I've recognized that, I give myself permission to ramble on, but I don't take anything I say seriously. I've also noticed that I'm more critical of myself and more impatient with others about one week prior to my period. I'll be walking down the street, yelling at myself, saying things like, 'I'm so fat, I can't believe it. You've been eating like a pig, won't you ever learn?' Suddenly, I'll realize, 'Gosh you're being extra tough on yourself,' and I'll quickly link it to where I am in my cycle. Sure enough, it's about one week prior to my period."

Another interviewee commented, "I'm notorious for criticizing myself before I go to sleep at night. I don't intentionally start off criticizing myself. It typically is the result of lying in bed reviewing my day. Several items will come up where I'll question the way I handled a particular employee. As a manager in the payroll department, I've got certain deadlines that I have to keep.

If I handle my employees poorly, you can see a difference in their performance. If I feel I haven't handled someone as well as I should have, I end up yelling at myself when I should be falling asleep. I'll say things like 'How could you be so stupid? What would your father say to you now? There, you've done it again! If Sandie doesn't do a good job on that report tomorrow, it's your fault.' It doesn't take a wizard to know that on those nights I have had a hard time getting to sleep. You'd think I'd stop criticizing myself." She adds laughingly, "But you know what I do—I start criticizing myself for the fact that I'm not falling asleep. That conversation can last for another ten minutes!"

Evaluate Content

It's important to get ourselves to the point where we can pay attention to our thoughts, determine when and where we tend to criticize ourselves, and look at this information with strict objectivity. We need to gather information and then start examining the quality and accuracy of the information we have collected.

Keep in mind that we need to be fair when we are criticizing ourselves. We would expect any other giver of criticism to be fair, but that's not always the case with self-criticism. We are our own worst enemy. If, as the giver, we are going to be unfair, then we need to rely on our good receiver skills for sorting out the quality and accuracy of our statements.

Poor self-criticism is best halted by asking ourselves the following four questions:

1. Who said this?
2. Where did I get this information?
3. Is it accurate?
4. Is it specific enough?

These questions reflect the receiver's flowchart (see page 29); some steps have been eliminated because of the unique nature of self-criticism.

Let's put these questions to use. We'll apply them toward types of situations in which we most commonly criticize ourselves.

What "Faults" Do We Criticize Ourselves For?

As we said earlier, nothing is off limits with self-criticism and it can occur at any moment, day or night. Still, there are some broad patterns of self-criticism that we can discern.

Things I "Ought to Have Done"

Survey results and individual interviews both revealed that many of us criticize ourselves for things we think we "should do." Take, for example, Marilyn. She is a thirty-two-year-old career woman who lives in Manhattan with her new husband, Jim. Her work requires that she be out of town a couple of days a week. Marilyn's friends kid her that she'd "better be careful because some good-looking woman might catch Jim's eye, and with the shortage of men and all . . ." Such comments can only get twisted into self-directed criticism and result in Marilyn's saying to herself, "You're wrong not to spend more time with Jim. Your friends are warning you that you are doing the wrong thing. You'll let him slip away." Or "You should stay home. Tell the client you can't come this week." Or "You should talk to your boss and tell him you don't want to travel as much."

Before Marilyn takes any action on this self-criticism, it's important that she step back and objectively examine what she is saying to herself. For instance, it's best if Marilyn analyzes *who says* that she needs to spend more time at home. Has Jim said anything? If not, *where did she get this information?* Furthermore, Marilyn needs to consider whether their marriage license specifies how many hours per week make for a happy relationship. Such a provision doesn't exist, so who says they have to spend more time together? She might answer that her friends told her, but how accurate would that information be?

At times, then, it's appropriate to ask whether we are justly criticizing ourselves. In Marilyn's case, before she continues to criticize herself any longer, perhaps it would be helpful if she reflects back to the expectations that she and Jim mutually established. For instance, it's no secret that Marilyn's work requires her to travel. Jim and Marilyn agreed that because of their present income needs, Marilyn *should* travel if her job demands it. Besides, both of them like to have some personal time to themselves. They also agreed that if at any point either of them felt uncomfortable with the arrangement, he or she would say something. Considering their mutually agreed-upon expectations, it is apparent that Marilyn's self-criticism is unwarranted. To further demonstrate the pointlessness of her self-criticism, Marilyn needs to ask herself, "Is criticizing myself for not spending enough time with Jim helping me achieve what I want?" The answer most likely is no. Marilyn needs to clarify what she wants. If Marilyn is like most career-minded women, what she really wants is to reconfirm her relationship with Jim and make sure that their "travel agreement" is still intact. Thus, Marilyn needs to take action and talk to him.

Things I "Ought Not Have Done"

One form of self-criticism is criticizing ourselves for things we should not have done—saying the wrong thing to someone, for instance. A professor may greet a new faculty member by saying, "It's good to meet you," when in fact they have met before. Or a husband may call his wife's boss by the wrong name. Or the president of an organization may acknowledge one of the company's most outstanding performers by discussing his role on a project that someone else actually handled.

In each of these cases, it's important to admit that you've made a mistake. Refusing to examine what we say or do and failing to admit our mistakes doesn't make them go away. Instead, they simply get pushed aside, and the feelings associated get buried and begin to fester. Openly admitting mistakes and acknowledging feelings make it easier to deal more realistically with situations such as these. If you determine that you can take action to rectify the situation, then do so. If you find you can't, then file away the experience so you can learn from it in the future, and let go of the criticism.

As Albert Ellis, the noted psychologist, has said, admitting our mistakes is natural, but mentally beating ourselves is unfair. And rather than waste energy questioning whether it's good or bad to beat ourselves mentally, a more useful question is, "Is this self-criticism helping?" Remember: The purpose of self-criticism is to point out negative aspects of ourselves and our behavior so that we can enhance our performance and promote our self-growth. Simply being hard on ourselves may be counterproductive, especially if the situation we are criticizing ourselves for occurs infrequently.

In addition to being brutally harsh, much self-criticism is disturbingly general: "I blew the whole thing." "I can't do anything right." "I made a mess of everything." These three statements alone have caused untold mental anguish.

We expect someone who is criticizing us to be specific, and we owe ourselves the same consideration. Of course, it's easy to generalize criticism.

For instance, someone who has had terrible problems with his Mustang may generalize that one bad experience and apply it to every car made by Ford. He will vow never again to buy a Ford car. Although he had only one bad experience, he is willing to apply generalities to the whole. When we criticize ourselves in this way, it's helpful to check out the accuracy of our self-criticism and ask ourselves whether the criticism is specific. If it isn't, try to make it specific. This will give you a better chance of dealing with the situation more realistically.

When We Say "I Can't Do It"

Sometimes we clutter our minds with critical statements about things we supposedly cannot do. For example: "I can't dance," "I can't play cards," "I can't tell jokes," "I can't remember people's names," "I can't understand computers," and so on. When you make such a statement, it's important to check out the source of the criticism. Ask, "Who says I can't? Where did I get this information? How old is it?"

Often we discover that we talked ourselves into the criticism. Checking out the accuracy of these statements causes us to look more closely at what is really being said. For example, if we say we can't do something, then it's important to sort out whether it's because we are incapable of doing it or because we don't want to. In either case, be sure the criticism is accurate and not the result of a distorted view of yourself.

Mistakes

We all criticize ourselves for the mistakes we've made. It's natural to do this, especially if we feel we haven't lived up to our expectations. But however disappointed we feel, it's important to listen to what we are saying. Remember that with self-criticism we're both the giver and the receiver. Therefore, we need to know what is being said and examine its accuracy. As with other forms of criticism, it's worthwhile to check out whether self-criticism is helping. Remember, the purpose of criticism is to point out what we are doing so that we can take appropriate action to help us achieve desired end results. Too often, we waste a lot of energy on criticizing ourselves instead of using that energy to determine whether any immediate and direct action can be taken.

As an example of someone who dealt well with self-criticism in a crisis situation, consider Kevin. Kevin, who lives in Kansas City, was in New York on a business trip. His meetings ran late the day of his return home. Hailing a cab, Kevin hurriedly asked the driver to take him to Newark Airport. Luckily, they arrived in record-breaking time; the only problem was that Kevin discovered he was at the wrong airport. His flight was departing from LaGuardia; in his haste, he had read the wrong portion of his ticket. Naturally, Kevin was upset. But rather than calling himself names and feeling sorry for himself, Kevin quickly recovered and focused on what he could do to catch a flight back home. Within five minutes, he had found out that another airline had a flight that was about to leave for Kansas City. Armed with his luggage, Kevin rushed to the next terminal and caught the flight in the nick of time.

You may conclude that Kevin only did the simple and obvious thing. Although there may be a good deal of truth to this assessment, in the heat of the moment, our emotions can easily overrule our ability to respond rationally. Keeping our emotions in check is best achieved by channeling the adrenaline produced by our aggravation into seeking out a viable solution.

Sometimes, however, our mistakes don't lend themselves to any direct action. Suppose you're walking down the street with a friend and you both decide to stop and buy a soft drink. You pay with cash from your wallet, and after walking for another mile, you suddenly notice that you've lost a twenty-dollar bill. Naturally, you're mad at yourself for making the mistake of losing the money. But the questions to ask yourself are: "Is yelling at myself helping? Is there anything I can do to rectify the situation?"

Perhaps you may learn something by examining the reason why you lost the twenty dollars, but chances are it's simply an error. If you can't take any action, simply let go of the situation. In all probability, all the self-criticism in the world won't recover your money.

If we continue to chastise ourselves mentally after determining that nothing can be done, we are wasting valuable energy and time. Criticizing ourselves at this point serves no purpose.

Personal Name-Calling

After we've made a mistake, it's easy to revert to saying negative things about ourselves, like calling ourselves stupid or dumb. This practice is called "personal name-calling," and it's a tough form of criticism because it seldom results in any positive benefit. Interestingly, many people in the study stated it is something they do automatically.

The next time you call yourself dumb or stupid, take notice. Ask yourself, "Who said that?" The answer is obvious—you did.

However it's helpful to remind yourself of this fact for two reasons. First, as both flowcharts (see pages 29 and 83) emphasize, it's important to determine the source of the criticism. Second, this question gives the receiver (you) the opportunity to stop and think about what is being said.

Once you have focused on what's been said, ask yourself whether your personal name-calling has been beneficial. If its purpose has been to relieve stress associated with making the mistake, chances are there are other less self-defeating means of accomplishing the same thing.

We could cite many examples to illustrate this point, but let's zero in on one incident that befell Lucy in her job as manager of a Chicago retail store. One of the salespeople came to her and asked for permission to leave early. At the time, Lucy was busily working on inventory control. For some reason, the interruption irritated her and, instead of calmly responding to the employee's request, she reacted angrily. She started yelling at the employee, saying things like, "All you want to do is ask me for favors. Why can't you just do your job and not ask for things?" After the salesperson left the office, Lucy realized her mistake. Instantly, critical thoughts flooded her mind and she berated herself for mistreating the salesperson.

But Lucy did not criticize herself for hours on end. Instead, she started to examine her thoughts. First, she asked herself whether blaming herself was helping, and she quickly confessed to herself that it was not; criticizing herself was only making her feel worse. Next, Lucy directed her thoughts to the source of the criticism. She assessed the situation by sorting out where and how she had acted ineffectively. After specifically identifying what she did wrong, Lucy asked herself if she could do anything about the situation and whether it was worth it. The answer to both these questions was yes. Immediately, Lucy decided what action was best to take. She decided to apologize to the salesperson for her outburst. When she apologized, Lucy wanted to make sure that she took full blame for the mistake. She also used this opportunity to let the employee know how much she appreciated her efforts and, of course, she granted her the time off.

Once she decided what she wanted and had plotted her strategy, Lucy let go of the mistake and the need to criticize herself.

If we were to review step by step what Lucy did, it would unfold as follows:

1. Realize that it's natural for stress levels to rise and for feelings of disappointment and anger to emerge after one makes a mistake.
2. Direct thoughts toward the source of the criticism.
3. Assess the situation.
   a. Identify specifically where you were not effective and what you did wrong.
   b. Determine whether you can do anything about each point.
4. Take action, if possible.
   a. Decide which action will have the greatest impact on achieving the desired end result.
   b. Develop your strategy and implement it.
5. If no action can be taken, just let go of the criticism.

When we criticize ourselves for the mistakes we've made and the things we should have done, it's important that we look beyond the hurt feelings. Seek out what lessons, if any, we can learn. It is critical to keep in mind that failures and mistakes are valuable learning opportunities, just as successes are. As a matter of fact, mistakes are probably better learning experiences than are successes. After all, when we make a mistake, the error pops right out at us and we can easily see what we must do to correct it. The reasons for success, on the other hand, are sometimes vague, and they may be difficult to identify.

In order to make optimal use of self-criticism, it's important that we be properly prepared for dealing with mistakes and perceived failures.

Learning to manage self-criticism involves letting go of the negative, self-defeating thoughts that shake our confidence and strip us of our ability to apply self-adjusting skills for staying in control.

As our example of the lost twenty-dollar bill showed, not every mistake lends itself to direct action to rectify the situation. When you can't take direct action, it's still advisable to go through the steps outlined above so that you may apply the insights you gain to a new situation. Working through each of the steps ensures that your mistake becomes a valuable learning experience. Your energies don't become fixed on what you did wrong; instead, they are redirected toward doing it right next time.

Participating in sports is a great way to learn from mistakes and to recover quickly. If a tennis player misses a shot, it's gone forever. But the insights that can be gained from studying why he or she missed the shot better prepares the player for the next one. The athlete develops a strong self-correcting mechanism. Interestingly, the more seasoned or experienced the athlete, the faster his or her self-correcting mechanism seems to operate.

The business world is also an excellent arena for learning from our mistakes. To illustrate this point, let's look at people in the selling profession. Because sales is such a competitive field, it is frequently likened to sports. Bill, a successful salesman for a computer company, says that every time he calls on a client, he imagines himself up at bat. The size of the sale determines how far he gets around the bases. If he misses the sale, he views it as an out. Before calling on his next prospect, Bill considers all aspects of the way he handled the previous sale and what he could have done better. He takes the approach that whenever he doesn't get a sale, it's a one-time mistake.

Typical of Bill's approach is the time that he realized, after an unsuccessful sales call, that his strategy could have been better. Rather than simply moving on after he lost the sale and figuring out on his own what went wrong, Bill decided to go back to the client and ask him why he didn't buy. His new strategy not only helped him learn firsthand what he could do better, but he also ended up hitting a triple with two strikes against him.

The important lesson to learn from Bill is that when you've lost a sale for reasons other than the customer's not wanting your product or service, you shouldn't let your mistakes scare you and lead you into a lot of worthless self-criticism. Turn it into a valuable learning experience instead.

Make pacts with yourself that give you permission to make

mistakes, provided that you turn them into learning experiences and take appropriate action.

Worry and Guilt

Worry and guilt deserve special attention not because they are common causes for self-criticism but because they are unfair: "Here you go again. You said you weren't going to worry and now look at you, worrying again." Or "Stop worrying," or "You shouldn't feel guilty," or "What are you feeling guilty for? It's so stupid," and on and on. It's unfair to criticize yourself for suffering guilt and anxiety, because these are emotions, and no amount of self-criticism can change them. To prove my point, have you ever stopped worrying after someone has told you, "Stop worrying"?

In my seventeen years in the stress field, I have observed that most Americans do not know how to stop criticizing themselves for worry and guilt. When they attempt to do so, they often compound the problem. To deal with guilt and worry more productively, we need to take a fresh look at these emotions.

First, there's nothing wrong with these feelings. Somewhere along the line, many of us learned to regard these emotions negatively. This could have originated in the late sixties, when everyone was supposed to be positive: if you were caught worrying, you weren't "in." But cultural attitudes aside, these emotional reactions serve a very healthy function. If we felt no guilt, every time we got angry at someone we would think nothing of striking that person. As Roger Depue, behavioral science chief at the FBI Academy, once told me, "Guilt helps to stop us from making the same mistake twice."

Worry plays a valuable place in our lives as well. It signifies the need for us to delve further and seek out either more or clearer information.

The best way to deal with worrying is the same strategy we prescribed for self-criticism: instead of berating yourself for worrying, ask what is causing the worry. Once you have identified the source of your worry, examine whether it's controllable and lends itself to any immediate action.

Let's consider a typical situation in which parents worry about their teenage daughter. The daughter had promised to be home by ten o'clock from a school-related activity that she had attended with a group of friends. Ten o'clock has come and gone, though she still hasn't come home. At 10:35, her mother tells her husband, "Sweetheart, I'm really worried. What do you think we should do?" The husband replies, "Stop worrying. She's probably got hung up at school over something and just hasn't been able to call. You know the school doesn't have many public phones." But the mother just sits there and frets.

This woman could learn to control her worrying by seeing it as a signal to get more information. Instead of letting her worrying get the best of her, she could ask herself, "What am I *specifically* worrying about?" Next, she needs to determine whether she can do anything about the situation. For instance, she could call her daughter's friends. She and her husband could even drive to the school to look for their daughter. A more drastic move would be to notify the police. Worrying is just a signal, and to deal with it effectively we need to investigate it further.

Sometimes we worry for the sake of worrying. If after examining the source of our worry, we discover that nothing can be done, then we need to let it go. We should use the same approach when dealing with guilt: analyze its source and take action if appropriate. If not, let it go. The quick charges we've discussed in earlier chapters are valuable techniques for "letting go" of worry—and guilt when appropriate.

Self-criticism is the only kind of criticism we have total control of. We have choices: how we give it, how we take it, and whether we make it work for us or allow it to debilitate us. We can choose to be our own worst enemy or we can learn to look at self-criticism as a valuable positive force that, used skillfully, can enhance our lives enormously. Harnessing self-criticism and making it work to our advantage is not, for most of us, a skill that comes easily. We must practice making ourselves consciously aware of what we are saying to ourselves and then react with candid objectivity. Many might find it helpful to begin by writing down the exact words and phrases used in moments of self-criticism. We must remember that the mind's eye witnesses dreams and fantasies as well as re-creates realistic pictures of past experiences. If we put our thoughts on paper, we can sometimes better assess their relationship to reality. By sorting out fact from fiction of what we say about ourselves, we can begin to truly learn from self-criticism.

Chapter 10

MAKING CRITICISM INTO A POSITIVE FORCE

You get it from strangers: "Move your car over, fatso. Do you think you own the whole road?"

You get it at work: "Terri, this report needs to be redone. You didn't include the budget reports from the development group. How could you have left them out?"

You get it from your children: "Mom, quit picking on me. You don't like the way I dress, you don't like my friends, you don't like my hair, you never have anything nice to say about me. You're always criticizing me."

You get it from your spouse: "Ted, I love you, sweetheart, but sometimes you are so insensitive. You know the best times to criticize me, because you know when it will hurt the most."

You get it from friends: "Agnes, I can't believe you're telling me this now. We've been friends for more than two years. You've never told me that you and Jack don't like playing cards with us. Why have you waited until now to tell me?"

Criticism is all around us. It is part of our daily life. It can be as subtle as a disapproving look from a passerby on a busy sidewalk or as direct as being fired from a job. To ignore criticism or to wish it away is not facing reality. Criticism is a vital part of our existence and if we understand and manage it well, it can empower each of us. As a misdirected force, it can be used to destroy people's careers, end relationships, take power and control over others, or erode a person's self-confidence. Yet, if understood and managed for positive ends, this same force can build confidence, promote the achievement of certain goals, and serve as a vital means for continual growth and inspiration.

DEVELOPING AN UNDERSTANDING OF CRITICISM

Using criticism as a positive force begins with understanding criticism and the different forms it can take.

Reading this book is a good first step for building the insights that are needed for establishing a solid understanding of criticism as both a giver and a receiver. Criticism is:

- A vital part of our life. No one is exempt at any age.

- A negative form of communication.
  No matter how hard we try to disguise criticism, whether by calling it positive feedback, constructive feedback, constructive criticism, or coaching skills, the content of criticism is *negative*.

- A powerful communication tool.
  Criticism, like praise, is nothing more than a communication tool designed to direct behavior in such a way that it will lead to the successful achievement of a desired end result.

- A source of information.
  Criticism is a highly charged form of information that is colored by our perceptions, our experiences, our different personalities and moods.

- Ultimately in the receiver's control.
  The receiver is ultimately in control of the criticism process. It's the receiver who colors the information, validates what is being communicated verbally and nonverbally, and decides whether it's acceptable and worthy of any action.

- A valuable tool for empowering self.

Self-criticism can be a valuable self-correcting system for assessing our behavior in order to discover better ways to achieve certain goals. If managed with finesse, self-criticism can be an inner source of strength that increases our self-confidence while at the same time provides us with opportunities for growth and improvement.

INTEGRATING CRITICISM INTO YOUR LIFE

Integrating criticism into our lives as a positive force is a skill that needs to be learned and then practiced. As with any skill, the most challenging step is putting it to use. Just as it exposes us to varying forms of success, it also exposes us to embarrassment, disappointment, and discomfort.

In an effort to make this step a positive learning experience, let's explore in more depth the way we approach the challenge of learning "new skills." Even though the skills sound familiar, they are new—not because we've never heard about them, but because we haven't used them before.

It's interesting to pay attention to how we view ourselves in the process of implementing these skills. For instance, some of us may decide to approach the use of these skills with the underlying belief that it will make us a better person. What's behind this approach is that something is wrong with us and by learning these new skills we will improve ourselves. Another approach stems from the premise of self-acceptance. It views the learning of new skills for handling criticism as something useful that can lead to greater effectiveness. The advantage of taking the latter approach is that if you are not totally successful, you will still view yourself as a good person. This particular view is preferred. Many of the interviewees, especially Dr. Albert Ellis, subscribes to this self-acceptance approach.

However, be aware that both approaches will lead to the same end result. The differences will most likely lie in the process. What's important is to recognize how you view yourself at the onset and throughout the learning process.

Don't Try to Do It All

Learning to handle criticism better by trying to improve on all fronts will surely cause disappointment and discouragement. There are two reasons for this. First, "trying" is not a strong enough commitment. As we all know, before a new skill becomes an integral part of our behavior, we first have to remember to use it. If we are only going to "try," chances are great that we will forget to implement it—after all, we only said we would try.

Second, disappointment and discouragement may result because of our desire to "do it all." It would be nice if we *could* do it all, but considering the number of demands we each face daily, it's easy to feel overwhelmed. The outcome is that the best of intentions rapidly die. So it's best to select one skill that you are committed to remembering to use on a regular basis. Also, when selecting that one skill, keep in mind the benefits you will gain. Adults are more apt to take on new challenges and stick with them if the energy expended is equal to or greater than the output. So choose your one skill carefully.

Don't Worry About Feeling Comfortable

As a result of working with individuals and groups over the past seventeen years, I'm amazed to observe how many people expect to feel "comfortable" while making changes in their behavior. It's as if feeling comfortable is linked with being successful. Therefore, if we feel uncomfortable during the learning phase, we are quick to be self-critical and possibly abandon the goal altogether.

It's unfair to think that you and others should feel comfortable when implementing the skills discussed in this book. It's unfair because whenever there is change, stress levels increase—that threatens the status quo. Things become more unpredictable. Besides having to do things differently, we are subjecting ourselves to possibly making more mistakes, while at the same time risking the fact that besides things getting better, they could potentially get worse.

Change in and of itself produces stress, but when you combine it with the expectation of having to feel comfortable, more stress is likely to be generated. So if feelings of discomfort arise while you are implementing these skills, remind yourself and others that the discomfort is natural and most likely due simply to *change*.

Don't Think of "from Now On"

More stress can be produced when we use the approach of "from now on." "From now on" assumes that once a goal has been set and communicated, it is fully functional from the outset. Operating from what I call the "from-now-on principle" is risky, because we are not always successful with each new attempt, especially at the beginning.

To minimize feelings of discouragement and the temptation of possibly abandoning the use of the new skill, it's valuable to give yourself and others "permission" to make mistakes, especially during the early learning phase.

When mistakes are allowed to occur, attempts to change behavior are less likely to turn into competitive matches. Married couples have been known to do this. It's almost as if some partners use criticism only for the purpose of keeping score and not for the purpose of directing behavior toward the achievement of goals. If one partner makes a mistake or forgets to do something, then the other partner is quick to accuse the mate of not caring or being incapable of keeping agreements. Taking this approach frequently results in both partners' losing their enthusiasm and their desire to pursue the goals they have set.

Don't get caught up in the principle of "from now on." Give yourself and others permission to make mistakes as the learning process unfolds. Among other things, making mistakes gives everyone involved great opportunities to practice using criticism positively.

GETTING STARTED

To identify the skill you want to focus on, you might try answering the following questions.

    1. Select which area is of greatest personal value.
        ☐ Giving criticism
        ☐ Receiving criticism
        ☐ Self-criticism
    2. Within that area, what would you like to do better?
    3. What benefit do you expect will result from using this skill?
    4. Will others notice a difference?
       Yes_____ No_____
       Please explain.

    5. How long are you willing to invest in learning to use the skill effectively?

(I'd recommend a minimum of seven days, and would encourage making a concentrated effort for as long as thirty days.)

    6. What would interfere, if anything, with your successful learning of this particular skill?

(Besides working toward a goal, it's valuable to honestly recognize what we do to ourselves that interferes with the successful accomplishment of the goal.)

    7. What steps can you take to help offset any of the above obstacles?

(Investing time and energy in answering this question is valuable because it puts you in in a proactive stance. Helping to offset any obstacles up front provides you with the energy you need to stay focused on the successful implementation of your goal.)

    8. On a daily basis you plan to_____.

(Breaking down your plan for taking action on a daily basis makes it easier for you to remember to implement the skill. At the same time, it clearly establishes your own built-in reward system.)

In an effort to help you get started, I've summarized below some important skills for you to refer to now and in the future.

Receiving Criticism

- Control lies with the receiver to sort out the criticism, validate it, and decide what action needs to be taken.
- Sort out, clarify, and evaluate the information being communicated by raising questions discussed in the receiver's flowchart (page 29).

Key questions to ask:

Will you accept criticism from this person? Is the criticism off limits?

Does the criticism have constructive value?

Is the criticism specific, and does it call for specific action?

This last question is probably one of the most important questions to ask. In our nationwide study on criticism, we discovered that respondents most frequently practice this skill of asking questions to make the criticism clearer and more specific. Next be sure to ask:

Will the action required of you fit your goals and objectives?

As the Simmons Market Research Bureau/Bright Enterprises study revealed, women show a tendency to change their behavior as a result of receiving criticism more frequently than do men.

Do you approve of the criticism?

This is another extremely important question to raise. You may want to give yourself a period of time to "cool off" before you consider it.

Do you have all of the information you need to take proper action?

- Don't let criticism wear you down. Remember to keep the big picture in mind and stay focused on what's most important.

The nature of the work and your position may involve criticism. If you work in a service job and if you are a manager, your work itself will invite criticism.

- Knowing yourself helps to prepare you for criticism.

The Simmons Market Research Bureau/Bright Enterprises revealed that criticism that questions our integrity hurts the most.

- Stress levels increase when you are being criticized. Be aware of this.

A number of factors can increase your stress, including personal thoughts.

- Avoid personalizing criticism by remembering to filter the information carefully—and "check it out" when necessary.

As our national study revealed, we tend to personalize criticism more from our mate than from anyone else we come in contact with.

- Keep stress levels under control by using quick charges and allowing the giver to finish what he or she has to say before responding.
- Keep in mind that it's worse to get no criticism than to get criticism.

Giving Criticism

- To give greater meaning and value to criticism, balance it with praise. People who always criticize others aren't taken seriously.

The nationwide study conducted by Simmons Market Research Bureau/Bright Enterprises showed that we tend to criticize our loved ones most frequently when we are tired or in a bad mood.

- Before giving criticism, be sure you know how the person prefers to be criticized. Are you going to criticize others the way they prefer to be criticized, or the way you want to?

The study showed that, interestingly, we are most unsure of how our boss and our in-laws will respond to criticism.

- Establishing clear expectations ahead of time builds a strong foundation that helps to minimize the receiver's likelihood of personalizing your criticism.
- Before giving criticism, be prepared to know how best to communicate with the person. If you are unsure, it may be best to postpone the delivery of criticism.
- Some people are more responsive when you incorporate visual, auditory, or kinesthetic sensory aids during communication.
- Before delivering criticism, know the type of action that the receiver needs to take. If you cannot identify a specific action, you may want to postpone giving the criticism.
- Before giving criticism, be sure you know individual goals as well as mutually shared ones. If you do not know what the shared goals and objectives are, then it's best to postpone or cancel giving criticism.
- During the mental rehearsal stage, be sure to take into account any preconceived notions that you may have regarding the other person. As we all know, if we enter into situations with prejudices, it will alter the way we come across and will have an effect on the final outcome.
- When giving the criticism, be sure to talk about the other person's behavior in relationship to your mutual goals and objectives. This is valuable because time is not wasted on excuses or trying to find fault with others.
- Getting started is easier when expectations about giving and receiving criticism have been discussed and agreed upon.
- Keep in mind that the research indicates that it is most difficult to start criticizing our boss, father, and friends.
- As you mentally rehearse how to deliver the criticism, if you question whether you are off limits, be sure to delay criticizing the other person until you are certain your comments are within bounds.
- Be sure that the criticism can be backed up. If specific examples are not available to support the criticism, it is best to delay or abort the criticism. The study revealed that, unfortunately, many of us tend to dump our stress on the ones we love the most—namely, our spouse and children. For instance, we are most likely to criticize our kids impulsively. When we do, we tend to forget to provide specific examples.
- If you want to effectively balance criticism with praise, be sure you know how to best reward the person in a way that is most meaningful.

- When delivering criticism, it's helpful to remind the person that you are not personally criticizing him or her, but a specific action.
- To enhance your effectiveness as the giver of criticism, be aware of how you react during the criticism process.

QUICK REMINDERS

- Be sure to listen carefully to the receiver.
- Pick the right time.
- Avoid criticizing the person in front of others, no matter how stressed you may be.
- Offer a solution, or work together to reach one.
- Use "we" statements appropriately and refer to the *issue* at hand without making reference to specific individuals.
- Work out a mutually agreed-on method for "letting go" of the criticism.
- Avoid asking the other person whether he or she understands. Instead, summarize together the key points of the discussion, perhaps in writing.
- Follow up after the criticism process has ended.

The key is to make sure that everybody keeps their part of the agreement.

NOTEWORTHY TACTICS AND SKILLS FOR SELF-CRITICISM

- If you are extremely good at beating yourself up, you can be just as good at working with yourself. If you consider the energies you expend on negative thoughts, all that is needed is to redirect those energies positively.
- Listen to what you say to yourself. Ask yourself, "If I had a friend who talked to me the way I talk to myself, would I still have him or her as a friend?"
- Listen to yourself in a nonjudgmental way. Interpret what you discover about yourself as "interesting."
- Be sure you are aware of the role that self-criticism plays in your life. Does it goad you into action? Is it a means of

discovering ways you can improve? Or is the role of criticism to discourage you to the point of not taking action?

- Put energy into sorting out and qualifying the accuracy of your self-critical statements.
- If you criticize yourself for things you "should do," ask yourself who said you "should do" them.
- If you spend a lot of time criticizing yourself for things you should *not* have done, remember you've already done them. Stay in the present and focus on what you want.
- If your self-criticism is generalized, remember to check it out for specifics. If you're unable to come up with supportable information, consider the criticism invalid. It could be that you are just tired or in a bad mood.
- If you've made a legitimate mistake, just remind yourself that you're not perfect—you're human. If you permit yourself to, you can learn a lot.
- If the mistake lends itself to no direct action toward a particular goal, give yourself permission to let it go.
- Remember, self-criticism is a valuable way to enhance your performance and promote good feelings about yourself.

SIGNS OF PROGRESS

As you practice implementing the skills of handling criticism, you may notice any one or more of the following changes in yourself.

Inner Strength
Investing energy into understanding criticism, and realizing that it can be managed, fosters an inner sense of strength. The feeling of being vulnerable and out of control becomes less intense. This helps to lower one's stress.

Greater Confidence
Inner strength is most likely associated with greater confidence. You approach situations with a freer feeling. Besides feeling more inclined to take on new challenges, there's a more intense belief that the goal will be achieved. More energy is directed toward

achieving a particular goal than it is on questioning why the goal can't be accomplished.

More Active Involvement

You are more likely to become willing to express ideas and get involved in activities that, beforehand, you might have let slip by. Part of the reason for allowing yourself to become more active might be linked to *truly* understanding that being criticized doesn't mean ending a particular pursuit. Quite the contrary; it's a way to point out what needs to be done to *continue* the pursuit.

Greater Commitment

Greater commitment seems to arise because you operate with the understanding that criticism is an ongoing part of life and that to be criticized for something doesn't automatically mean you are bad.

As Betsy King, one of our country's leading golf professionals has found, all that matters is that you do your very best. Even if you don't win, you've still utilized your skills and talents to the best of your ability—and what more can you ask of yourself?

Better Ability to Learn from Self and Others

When you're able to manage criticism, whether you are a receiver or a giver, criticism isn't threatening. You'll find that you are better able to look for valuable insights that will help you to achieve an end result. In the process, a nice thing happens— relationships tend to be strengthened, as trust and acceptance are exchanged.

Willingness to See the Humor in Situations

It's great to be able to laugh at yourself naturally. The first time you do it, it's almost as if you question if it's really you. Within a very short period of time, it becomes loose and free. It doesn't mean that whatever has occurred is any less significant. Instead, the laughing is related to self-acceptance and the acknowledgment that in the overall scheme of things, the event isn't all that important.

Laughter is even more exhilarating when you can get someone else to see how ridiculous or trivial a situation is. The laughter gets you over the hurdle more quickly, and you're able to easily regain your focus on what's most important.

Greater Understanding of Criticism and the Impact It Can Have on Others

As a parent or an authority figure, you will tend to pay more attention to how you actually give criticism and the purpose it is to serve. If the purpose is anything less than constructive, you may be more apt to postpone or cancel the criticism.

Working at Being Your Own Best Friend

Because criticism is such an integral part of each of our lives, it's a wonderful—if, at times, extremely painful—feeling to know you're using it to develop an honest relationship with yourself. If you can do that, then all the criticism you've given and received will have been worthwhile.

Let's face it, there's no escaping criticism. It is unquestionably a part of our lives. However, after reading this book you may have better insight into how to take the power inherent in the negativity of criticism and direct it in ways to achieve desired end results, and greater fulfillment in life.

APPENDIXES

Appendix I:

ON THE FIRING LINE: WHAT WOULD YOU DO?

It hasn't been the best of mornings. Your train stalled between stations for half an hour. So you were late for your 9:00 A.M. meeting. The coffee machine on your floor is broken, and you're dying for some caffeine. And your secretary's called in sick. Now you're sitting at your desk. The phone rings. It's Cecilia, a manager in Personnel—and the hesitant tone of her voice alerts you to the fact that she's not comfortable with what she's about to say. You know your day is going to take a turn for the worse.

"Gene, you need to be aware that Larry [one member of the eight-man production team you manage] just left my office. He's quite unhappy with his present situation in your department. He told me bluntly that he feels as if you and the others don't like him. For example, he says you'll say hello to everyone else but that you look away whenever you pass him in the hallway. He just doesn't feel he's a part of the team.

"I don't know what you're planning to do about this, Gene," Cecilia concluded, "but I guess you'll have to do *something*. Larry's asked that his comments be added to his Personnel files. Good luck." As you hang up the phone, startled and perturbed, one thought flashes across your mind: "How am I going to resolve this?"

Let's put *you* "on the firing line" as we explore everyday incidents in which criticism is either offered or received. To benefit most from the examples we've chosen, try to put yourself in each protagonist's situation, and ask yourself the following questions:

- How would I handle myself if this were happening to me?
- What have I learned about giving and receiving criticism that's applicable?
- Has anything similar ever happened to me? What mistakes or smart moves did I make in resolving the problem?

Try to be as honest with yourself as you can. Keep in mind that with each of these incidents, there are no right or wrong answers, only *better* ones.

And now, back to Gene and his disgruntled staffer, Larry.

Gene personalized Cecilia's criticism. His interpretation of the call was that he was being criticized for failing to integrate his employee properly into the social fabric of the department. Unsure of his next move, Gene discussed the matter with his boss, who advised him to take no action at all. "This company is not set up to solve personal problems. We're not a counseling service, and it's not *your* job to make sure that Larry is well liked. We're here because we have a job to do. It's up to Larry to integrate with his colleagues successfully." Concluding, the boss reiterated that the issue was of no significant consequence.

The point here is *not* whether you agree or disagree with Gene's boss. By referring to the receiver's flowchart (page 29), we find that the boss simply examined the nature of the criticism and determined that the criticism was off limits because his managers were not required to be social directors.

Putting yourself in Gene's position, would you have perceived that Personnel was criticizing your management style? If so, refer to the receiver's flowchart. Did you conclude that it was inappropriate for Cecilia to be dealing directly with Larry? If you did, you might take the following action, which is exactly how Gene handled it: Schedule a meeting with Personnel to request that if incidents such as this occur in the future, Personnel should suggest that the employees bring their grievances to the boss directly.

This action prevents managers from having to deal with "hearsay" criticism, which is far more complex to resolve.

Would you also go directly to the disgruntled employee? Gene did. This allowed him to publicize his position regarding staff complaints about departmental interpersonal operations. As a boss, you might also suggest to Larry that he should approach you first, before bringing any grievances to Personnel. Furthermore, you might remind him that the only action Personnel could possibly take would be to tell you, the boss, about your employee's complaint. Suggest to Larry, then, that you would have appreciated an opportunity to resolve the issue between yourselves. Subsequently, if Larry still felt stymied, he would be justified in bringing the matter to the attention of others.

In a one-on-one with Larry, Gene addressed the nature of the complaint and attempted to clarify Larry's intention in bringing the matter to Personnel. Did Larry genuinely intend to offer legitimate criticism (which has the underlying expectation that an action will be taken)?

In the course of discerning whether Larry was delivering a "complaint"—i.e., "grumbling"—or offering a criticism, you might also remind him that cultivating a pleasurable social life is not a priority item. What *is* expected of employees is that they work diligently at their job responsibilities and, if necessary, at "fitting in" socially with the rest of the players.

As you have probably concluded, bringing this incident to your boss's attention—as Gene did—may not have been necessary. Gene's boss quickly labeled the affair "trite," but perhaps his unspoken message to you may have been that this was not an issue significant enough to involve him. Instead, this was your *management* dilemma to resolve, and he would have preferred you handle it directly.

Responsible follow-up to Larry's complaint was Gene's managerial dilemma, and like Larry, he made some mistakes as he struggled to resolve it. In the process, both men learned important new concepts about giving and receiving criticism.

Let's now examine an example of unsolicited and misdirected criticism. Jay is the golf pro at an exclusive southern country club. His responsibilities include managing the pro shop; proper maintenance of the equipment; giving lessons and helping to increase membership. Jay is one of the club's most visible and accessible employees, so it's understandable that members frequently engage him in lengthy conversations about what they generally dislike about the club even though it has nothing to do with Jay's area of responsibility.

Just the other day, Maryellen Rodgers ran into Jay at the clubhouse and launched her sorry tale: "Jay, I'm just fed up. You've got to do something about the service in the main dining room! The waiters are all inexperienced and unconcerned. You sit at a table for ten minutes before you're even handed a menu.

"And the new lifeguard at the pool—he's nothing short of abusive. I've seen him yell at some children who have burst into tears afterward! How dare he speak so harshly to them? Frankly, I'm surprised more mothers haven't complained."

If you were Jay, how might you respond to Mrs. Rodgers— knowing that you have absolutely nothing to do with the waiter service or lifeguard functions at the club? Let's take a look at the evolution of two possible responses to Mrs. Rodgers's legitimate but misdirected criticisms.

One response might be as follows: "Mrs. Rodgers, those are important issues and I'm glad you feel comfortable enough to discuss them with me. However, those aren't my areas of responsibility; I only handle the pro shop. You need to discuss this with Mr. Hargrove. He's the club's general manager, you know."

Response #2, which follows, is what we prefer. Jay responded, "Thanks for bringing all this to my attention, Mrs. Rodgers. If you have a minute, let me get my pen and I'll record what you've said. Then I'll pass this on to Mr. Hargrove. I'm sure he'll appreciate your criticisms."

At this point, Maryellen—somewhat abashed—said, "Oh, Jay, there's no need to bother Mr. Hargrove with all this. I guess I just needed to get some things off my chest. I'm sure the situation isn't as bad as I've made it out to be."

There's also a third way to handle Mrs. Rodgers. Jay could have responded, "Mrs. Rodgers, thank you for telling me all this. I really don't have responsibility for the pool or the dining areas, but what I'd suggest you do is write down your criticism in a letter at your convenience and send it directly to me. I'll make sure Mr. Hargrove gets it. Or, better yet, write to Mr. Hargrove yourself, and tell him that you've already discussed the matter with me."

Why is this also a preferred response? Because even though Maryellen Rodgers is "off limits" with her criticisms to Jay, he recognizes that he is in the service industry. His job is to provide top-notch services to club members, and, as such, his responsibilities are greater than his immediate purview of the pro shop and the golf tournaments. Satisfied members make for a thriving club and, ultimately, for a securely employed golf pro!

As successful politicians realize when holding public service jobs, you cannot afford to forget that your customer is The Public. As cumbersome and demanding as it may be at times, you must remain focused on what your job is. It's easy to get bogged down in paperwork or in company infighting, but if your job is to please the public, no criticism may be viewed as off limits.

Remember, there are several different methods for responding to unsolicited criticism. It is important to listen intently and show an interest in the person as you determine the critic's intention. With very little effort, you can offer support and deflect negative energy by staying focused and sincerely offering to be of help.

Here's another chance to practice handling unsolicited criticism. The following situation happened to a good friend of mine who is the executive director of a state newspaper association. His role is all-encompassing: while his primary task is to serve newspaper owners and publishers across the state by coordinating efforts for lobbying representation in Washington, he also is involved in a host of community-oriented, educationally active programs.

My friend is well known in the community in which he lives—but the specifics about his job functions are less well known. Public perception is that he holds a very important and influential job in the all-powerful newspaper industry. Because of my friend's highly visible position, he is frequently approached by citizens who want to get something off their chests.

He told me recently that one afternoon, while at lunch, a prominent local businesswoman, whom we'll call Elizabeth Diaz, approached his table and interrupted him in the middle of a sentence, saying, "I just don't know what's going on with reporters today. They take a simple little incident and blow it way out of proportion. Look at what they've said about my company in today's paper! It's total misrepresentation. Something's got to be done about it. It's just not fair."

Once again, put yourself in my friend's position. How would you have handled such a situation? Let me suggest two different responses, and we'll analyze the merits and drawbacks of each.

Response #1: "Elizabeth, I can relate to what you're saying—in fact, I hear it all the time. But, really, you're talking to the wrong guy. You ought to be lodging this complaint with Peter Hunter. He's the paper's editor-in-chief and I'm sure he can take some action for you. By the way, how's the company doing? I read your annual report and . . ."

Response #2: "Elizabeth, I'm glad you brought this up. Even though handling reporters is not my job per se, I'd be glad to look into the situation for you. Would you care to draw up some specifics in a formal letter and send it to me? I'd be glad to make sure that it gets into the proper hands."

Experience has proven that #2 is, by far, the wiser choice. Although Elizabeth's criticism was truly off limits for my friend, he's learned from similar experiences that confrontations can be avoided by patiently listening to the person and showing respect for his or her point of view.

Furthermore, my friend told me that the point is not really whether the criticism is valid or not; rather, it's making sure that the responsibility of the complaint remains with the originator.

It is this perhaps hard-learned philosophy that prompted my newspaper friend to suggest tactfully that Elizabeth formally write out her complaints. Experience has shown that people will rarely follow through. "Most people," said my wise newspaper friend, "simply want the courtesy of being heard. And that is the greater duty of my job as a prominent member of the service industry."

With organizations taking on a lean and mean attitude, many employees have had to face the stresses associated with downsizing. As it so happens, the company where you work is faced with a similar dilemma.

As a manager of operations, you are obliged to conduct exit interviews for those employees whose jobs are being eliminated. One of the challenges you face is that most of the employees that you'll be interviewing have been with the company at least fifteen years; you have been an employee for only five years. After each meeting, you are to direct the people to a human resources representative, who will explain the information pertinent to the separation package offered by the corporation: savings plan distribution, career planning outplacement activities, and insurance benefits.

Let's zoom in on an upcoming exit interview that you'll be having with Sam, an employee who's been with the company for over eighteen years. What's special about this interview is that besides knowing Sam for the past five years, you were responsible for his last promotion. This discussion will be painful for both of you.

As his boss, how do you best approach Sam?

I hope that before you focus your energies on what you are actually going to say to Sam, you consider whether or not you are properly focused and well prepared for this meeting. Let's discuss the importance of being prepared in depth.

Bill Linderman, vice-president and director of corporate training and development at a major commercial bank in New York, says, "From my experience, being prepared is of utmost importance and something managers commonly overlook." He's noticed that many managers simply jot down a few key things to say just prior to going into the meeting. Typically, these meetings turn into an extremely uncomfortable event for both the manager and the employee being dismissed.

Postmeeting exit interviews that Bill Linderman has conducted revealed that people being dismissed didn't understand the reason they were losing their jobs. Others complained that their managers were rude and offensive when explaining the circumstances.

To minimize the chances of having the meeting turn into an angry session in which individuals are verbally attacked, it's best to be properly prepared.

Bill Linderman recommends that every manager prepare for the exit interview by sticking close to the following three goals:

1. Maintain the person's self-esteem.
2. Ensure open communication.
3. Focus on resolution of issues.

If a manager loses sight of any of these goals, the meeting is less effective.

Maintaining self-esteem is of utmost importance. It means knowing something about Sam, the experience that he's had, his length of stay with the company. How is he likely to react to the news? Will he take it as personal criticism? Is he marketable? Does he feel as if this is a good opportunity to break away? As Bill Linderman emphasizes, in a sensitive situation like this, "It's crucial for a manager to protect a person's self-esteem; otherwise the manager has failed at effectively delivering the message."

If the manager does not listen well and fails to keep lines of communication open, it is very difficult to resolve the important issues at hand, that is, explaining the business reason for eliminating the position and why Sam was chosen as someone to be eliminated as opposed to someone else.

Planning what you are going to say is extremely important in a situation like this, because an employee's irrational or unpredictable response can easily cause the meeting to go astray. In an effort to prepare managers, Bill Linderman developed and successfully implemented a discussion model that covers five major topics:

1. Purpose of the meeting
2. Business rationale

3. Human resources support
4. Next steps
5. Closing the meeting

Prior to the meeting, managers will fill in key points to cover under each item. The model easily helps the manager stay focused.

As a matter of fact, it's not uncommon for many managers to actually keep the model visibly in front of them during the entire meeting with the employee.

To prevent difficulties from getting started, Phyllis White, division manager of human resources at American Management Association, says, "From my experiences both at American Management Association and at Saks Fifth Avenue, where I was director of personnel, I've learned that it is best to get to the point right away. When you are clear and honest from the beginning of the meeting, you build credibility.

"Once the situation has been presented to the employee," continues Phyllis White, "it's important to address any concerns that might exist. However, at some point, it's necessary to move the meeting along."

Because a meeting like this is inherently uncomfortable, experience has shown that it's valuable to close the meeting by reviewing the issues and concerns that were raised. It's important that the employee understand what has been said before you close the meeting on a supportive note. For instance, Bill Linderman's model suggests closing the meeting by saying something like, "I realize that this may be a difficult time for you, and you should know that an extensive support system has been established to help you during this transition period."

Having the model, such as the one suggested by Bill Linderman, is useful because it helps clarify the manager's role, which is not to affront the employee or to come across in a critical way.

Here's a familiar sales situation. Decide how you would go about improving your sales performance if you were in David's place:

David has been a sales rep for a medium-sized manufacturing

firm for the past ten months. He's one of nine reps who cover the eastern and southern United States. Unfortunately for David, his sales performance for the past two months has not met the company's requirements.

David's initial reaction is to blame others for his lack of sales—his sales manager, the topsy-turvy economy, hot weather, and poor leads.

This self-protective thinking will ultimately backfire, and David's already shaky self-esteem will suffer even more. By falsely reassuring himself that "no one could perform well under these circumstances," David will emerge the loser.

Such intricate self-imposed intrapersonal mental games tend to center on believing various excuses and accusations of one sort or another in an effort to avoid the risk of a setback that seems even more threatening. David avoids facing failure by living an illusion. We all do this at one time or another—but when we play mental games to avoid failure in significant areas of our lives, the consequences can be devastating. David is jeopardizing his job and has nothing to gain by making excuses and blaming others for his poor performance. His only gain is a temporary one. He might maintain his self-esteem, but he risks losing his job.

As is the case with many sales professionals, David needs to be reminded that he was not hired to identify problems and be overwhelmed by them but, rather, to creatively overcome those problems with good ideas and solid implementation strategies. That reality of the job may be why the best salesmen never stop when they hear their first "No" from a potential client. That "No" is instead interpreted as an indication that the client just doesn't have enough backup information to say "Yes!" "No" becomes a challenge, not a signal to stop trying because of fear of failure or loss of self-esteem.

Likewise, it would not be wise for David to go to his sales manager and blame his poor sales performance on lack of good training and supervision. Even if his assessments of management and the sales training program were accurate, it's important to take into account the nature of "unspoken expectations." For instance, it's unlikely that management will listen to sales reps who are nonperformers. Management listens to those who are successful and dedicated to making things happen.

Instead, David would be better off going to his boss and asking for guidance. Again, another unspoken expectation is operative. The unspoken expectation is that if a sales manager is going to take time to "coach" a salesperson, then it better result in a lot of activity. If the sales rep does nothing to help himself, then it's predictable that the sales manager will not be anxious to help a second time. David needs to focus his energies on taking "action" even when he doesn't feel like it and he must learn from his errors. It's well known in the selling profession that great salespeople aren't born—they're made.

Here's one situation that's bound to strike a chord in most women. A mother and daughter have decided to spend the day together, clothes-shopping. Mother's very anxious about receiving a positive reaction from her fashion-conscious daughter as she tries on numerous outfits.

Usually the daughter is supportive of her mother's choices, and tends to make such comments as "I really like the way your skin glows when you wear that color," or "That suit was *made* for you! It fits so well." But today she's afraid to say anything at all, for fear of sounding overly critical. *Everything* her mother has tried on so far is dreadful!

Sensing her unspoken opinions, the mother presses her on the last dress: "What's the matter, honey; you're so silent! Can't you tell me honestly what you think of how I look?"

There are a number of responses you can offer at this point. Remember, your mother deserves a response, and an honest one, at that. Put yourself in this daughter's shoes. What would honest feedback consist of?

An excellent response would be something like, "It's just the dress, Mom; it's not you."

"Well, I just don't like it" leaves the receiver feeling frustrated and possibly hurt, because the intention behind the criticism is unclear. Furthermore, it's difficult to learn from this type of criticism because it lacks an explanation as to what led to the giver's conclusion and eventual offering of criticism.

In this case, though, the daughter delivered a message that was requested and received—with good feelings all around. By keeping these insights in mind the next time you go shopping with your mother, chances are great that it will be a pleasurable time.

Alicia, a new product manager, has been on the job for only a few months. Leo, one of the staff members who now reports directly to her, is overdue for a performance review.

Alicia's predecessor actually completed writing Leo's review before he left, but for some reason unknown to Alicia, he had neglected to give Leo his review. The former boss had given Leo a very poor performance rating—barely average—and he recommended that there be no salary increase this year. Among other factors, he cited an inability on Leo's part to pay attention to details while keeping the big picture in mind.

This would mean that for the first time in his six-year history with the company, Leo wouldn't get a salary increase. Alicia's boss wants her to conduct the review even though she's only been in that position for a short time and cannot appreciate the full scope of Leo's overall performance. Nor does she have the perspective needed to determine whether his performance over the past year shows a marked decline from previous years.

Imagine you are Alicia. You wonder whether Leo's former boss's appraisal may be inaccurate. Yet you are being pressured to schedule the review. How would you handle the situation?

Without delay, let's see exactly what happened. Alicia called Leo into a private meeting and said, "The following performance appraisal is based on direct comments from your former boss." Then, point by point, Alicia walked Leo through his less-than-satisfactory review. When Alicia concluded with the words "So we've decided to hold back on a salary increase for you this year, Leo," the enraged staffer exploded. "I presume there's nothing more for us to discuss," he stormed at Alicia. Unable to muster a reply, Alicia pulled her files together, stood up, and left the room two steps ahead of Leo. In short, the meeting was a disaster.

As soon as Alicia was out of earshot, Leo repeated the conversation to everyone whom he encountered. Having thus divided the department into two camps—"pro-Leo" and "pro-Alicia" (whose ranks were small indeed!), Leo marched into Personnel and issued a formal protest. After a week of intense lobbying efforts, Leo's raise was finally approved.

Two years later, when I met Alicia and she related the above incident to me, she admitted that she was still upset over the way she handled the situation.

Once again, try to put yourself in Alicia's position. Refer to the giver's flowchart (page 83) and, knowing that you can neither delay nor abort the criticism, ask yourself what you might have done differently.

If you arrive at a conclusion similar to the following, you have a solid understanding of the manager's role plus a good sense of how best to offer criticism under difficult circumstances:

As you prepare to discuss Leo's performance appraisal, it becomes evident that you cannot support such negative criticism. At the same time, you don't know Leo well enough to be able to predict how he reacts to criticism. And, most important, you are unsure of exactly what type of response behavior you wish to elicit from Leo.

Prior to meeting with Leo, it's important for you to discover the best approach for criticizing him. This can be accomplished by querying others with whom he has worked for years. You can also ask Leo directly, "With which bosses in the past did you most enjoy working? What irked you, if anything, about even your favorite boss's criticism style?" His answers would provide you with valuable insight for forming a more congruent working relationship.

Because you are, at this point, still unable to validate criticism from Leo's former boss and because you obviously want Leo to maintain a high-quality performance level, you may want to try another way of resolving this impasse, especially if you gain the support of your boss: negotiate an agreement whereby Leo is granted an additional six months to "prove" himself to you. If his performance meets all standards, you would recommend that he receive a retroactive salary increase.

Another approach would be to meet with Personnel and your immediate supervisor and fight for a minimal raise, effective immediately, on the ground that it's only fair to give a six-year employee the benefit of the doubt, with the understanding that you'll be supervising him closely.

Preparing for the meeting with Leo means making sure that you keep a proper focus. Talking about past performance griev-ances with the old boss is not as worthwhile as seizing an oppor-tunity to move forward and discuss present issues. It means clarifying expectations about his job responsibilities; the quality of work desired; and how the two of you might begin to work most effectively together as a team. Perhaps this meeting could become the first of several, regularly scheduled, wherein a dia-logue pertaining to these issues is ongoing. To do this effectively, in a manner that serves both you and Leo, requires that a certain level of objectivity be maintained. At the same time, you must each express a sincere willingness to work with one another for mutually beneficial results.

This initial meeting (and any subsequent ones that follow) is not intended to be used to rehash who's right and who's wrong. You must afford Leo as much time as he needs to respond to your comments—especially the negative ones. After all, this will be the first time he learns that management is displeased with his performance.

Because the meeting is highly sensitive, you would be correct in establishing some guidelines up front. For example, using your own words, you might want him to know how much time there is available for the meeting and the fact that whatever is discussed will remain private and will not be broadcast outside the meeting room. Reiterate that your intention is not to assign fault but, rather, to pass along an evaluation of Leo's performance over the last year for the purpose of establishing mutual expectations and goals.

You might conclude your opening remarks by saying, "I want

this meeting to end with you feeling good about this department and your role as a team player. We will have raised important issues and we will have set a direction that we will strive toward. So let's agree now not to leave this room until we've had an open discussion that we both understand and have ultimately agreed upon."

Once these guidelines have been communicated and mutually agreed on, it will be primarily up to you—the boss—to ensure that they are adhered to.

It's unfortunate that this incident left Alicia with more than a bad memory. For the next ten months, she was forced to contend with an embittered staffer. Lucky for both of them, Leo moved on to another firm within the year. Had the incident been handled a little differently, perhaps they could have had the chance to create an environment in which each could share in a tremendous opportunity for on-the-job maturation and growth.

Daniel and Ray worked together for five years before Daniel promoted Ray to his first management position. Ray had a reputation for being one of the finest service technicians on the staff of the phone company where they were employed. As a new manager, Ray had equally high aspirations.

His new job required Ray to manage twenty-one technicians in their most active region. Corporate headquarters was also situated in his new province. Daniel made it clear that Ray's number-one priority was to reduce the amount of "downtime" of their most highly sophisticated computer systems.

Ray worked very hard in his new managerial position. He was eager to learn all he could about departmental operations and he insisted on throwing himself into every technical problem that arose. As a result, in no time at all, Ray was putting in twelve-hour days, six days a week. He maintained this high-energy pace for the first four months.

However, as the weeks wore on, Ray began to realize that departmental energy levels—as well as his own—were dropping as it became apparent that results weren't equivalent to output. Daniel also noticed over the four-month period that, in addition to sluggish departmental performance, Ray's attitude had begun to change. Instead of being optimistic and solution-oriented, Ray had become irritable and discouraged.

Several more months passed with no end in sight to this downward spiral. Daniel now knew he would have to tell Ray that because his group's performance level was not adequate, Ray would have to be reassigned to a less visible, less problem-intensive area where he would have a smaller group reporting to him.

As Ray's manager, how would you go about informing him of this "demotion"?

Daniel was both a fair and a willing manager. Prior to meeting with Ray, he reviewed the giver's flowchart (page 83) to ensure proper preparation. For example, Daniel understood that he not only needed to clarify Ray's goals, he also needed to take into consideration how his criticism might affect Ray.

Having worked so closely together for more than five years, Daniel knew that Ray preferred one-on-one meetings at the end of the day outside the workplace. Daniel also knew that Ray typically personalized criticism, turning business issues into personal ones. Last, Daniel knew that Ray was a visual thinker and that he would grasp more if Daniel provided some visual aids to increase levels of understanding during the meeting.

Mentally rehearsing the meeting made it easier for Daniel to express himself calmly and wisely. His intention was to be honest with—and genuinely help—his friend and associate.

The talk was planned for 5:30 one afternoon at a favorite after-work bar-restaurant. Positioning themselves at a quiet table, Daniel began a light conversation about shared past experiences and the quality of a relationship that had been established over a number of years. He then took out a sheet of paper and drew for Ray one half of the congruency model (page 114). Daniel talked a bit about his strong personal as well as his professional feelings for Ray.

Then Daniel tactfully shifted the conversation with the sentence, "Ray, what we're really here to talk about is *not* a negative thing." He told him that he was being reassigned to a less pressured region, and he explained that this wasn't necessarily a bad thing because new managers need time to get the basics under their belt before going on to more active arenas.

Daniel took responsibility for some of Ray's "failures" by acknowledging that the assignment he'd been given was probably far more complex than any one person could manage, especially someone so new at the job. He also regaled Ray with some of his own early less-than-perfect attempts at managing, since he, too, had a technical background and had come up through the ranks. Throughout the conversation, Daniel consistently related everything back to Ray's personal goals, at the same time simultaneously reinforcing how he personally and professionally respected and accepted his colleague.

The outcome of the meeting, as you may have guessed, was remarkably positive. To ensure that Ray would receive the training he sorely needed, Daniel promised to arrange for Ray to attend a series of in-house management-training seminars that the company was offering. He also set about hiring a management consultant to work with Ray periodically to refine and reinforce certain personal skills, as well as to implement and apply the new management concepts he was learning. As a matter of fact, Daniel had wanted to do this from the beginning, but because of Ray's initial reluctance, combined with the demands of a heavy work flow, he allowed the idea to slide.

Daniel also agreed to spend more quality time with Ray, teaching him to prioritize work and to "coach" him whenever necessary.

While I am sure that Ray left the meeting feeling on some level that he'd "failed," it is equally apparent that he must have felt some sense of relief and anticipation because he knew that taking over a smaller region would give him an opportunity to learn the basics of good management without being overwhelmed. This is one shining example of a manager's criticism style that ought to be emulated by those in leadership positions.

Here's an interesting example that illustrates how smart it can be to discuss office problems with people who aren't directly involved. Mike and Richard have been good friends for years. Mike can remember way back when Richard, an account rep, first joined the advertising agency of which he's currently a managing partner. And similarly, Richard recalls Mike's struggling days in law school and his first clerkship with a renowned federal judge.

During one of their frequent weekend get-togethers, Richard brings up a troublesome office situation that involves Sharon, their studio manager, who's been in that position for a year.

Let's listen as Richard explains his dilemma to Mike: "One of Sharon's responsibilities is to call free-lance artists and arrange for them to come at short notice to work on special projects with tight deadlines.

"Every time I brief her on what we need done and whom she might consider hiring, she resists. It's as if she is mentally criticizing me. I can imagine her thinking, 'Damn that Richard! Here he comes looking for me to bail him out. He asks for the impossible every day, at the last possible minute.'

"Frankly, what goes on in *my* mind is, 'Sharon, if I can bust my chops working on an account till eleven P.M. for two weeks straight, you can pick up the damn phone and bring in some free-lancers by the end of the day!' You know, Mike, my feeling is that she *tries* to get the job done, whereas I *expect* her to do it."

At this point, Mike queries his friend, "Rich, have you said anything to her specifically about this impasse?" Rich responds, "Well, to tell you the truth, just the other day I saw that irritated look on her face and I decided to remind her that the agency is client-driven and that our job is to do whatever our clients request. Then I said, 'Sharon, if you can't stand the heat, get out of the kitchen.'

"You know, Mike, I just don't know what to do about her. If it were anyone else, it wouldn't be a problem: she'd be out the door. But she's well respected and admired by her staff and by clients— and I genuinely want to resolve this thing."

"How else have you tried to communicate with Sharon?" asked Mike. Richard thought for a moment and replied, "Whenever her turnaround time is especially good, I always thank her and tell her how much the effort was appreciated." "Do you ever get back to her and tell her about the final outcome of the campaign?" Mike continued. "Not really," Rich responded. "That might be a valuable tool for you," Mike commented. "You know, people appreciate knowing how their efforts contributed to a successful final outcome.

"Let me ask you another question," Mike went on. "Have you noted any improvement in Sharon's performance since you and she have been having these confrontations?" "Not really," Rich confessed. "I have some ideas," Mike told him.

What suggestions might you offer Rich in this case? As you read along to find out what Mike actually recommended, would you find Mike's manner helpful or patronizing?

Here's what Mike suggested: "First of all, I'd get the two of you out of the office to talk about your problem. Why not invite her to lunch next week? Then, focus the conversation on three items. The first is to make sure she has a good grasp of the big picture. Maybe no one's told her about how incredibly competitive your industry is—or how especially demanding the clients are that are attracted to your agency.

"Furthermore," Mike proceeded, "I'd make sure Sharon fully understands your role in the agency. Everyone may not be aware that in your capacity you are seen as the 'troubleshooter.' Problems hit your desk at the very last minute and you are forced to react and to make on-the-spot policy decisions. Maybe Sharon just thinks you're disorganized and that if you could manage your projects better, your last-minute confrontations with her would stop. So why don't you make sure she understands completely what your job is all about? Maybe then she won't interpret your directives as personal attacks.

"The only other thing I'd suggest," Mike concluded, "is that you consider being honest with Sharon and talking about possible ways in which the two of you could learn to work better together."

Richard, recognizing wise counsel when he heard it, immediately put Mike's ideas to work. At first, Sharon was wary of his lunch invitation but recognized a need to be open to a dialogue.

Now, Sharon and Richard meet regularly on Monday mornings to assess strategy and to review the upcoming week's priority assignments. These days, when Richard informs Sharon of yet another last-minute problem that needs to be resolved, her first inclination is not to be defensive, it's to be cooperative, and to genuinely want to handle the assignment with grace and good will.

The smooth working relationship now enjoyed by Richard and Sharon owes a great deal to Mike's sensitive perception of both the situation and his ability never to lose sight of whom he was talking to. Mike never came across as patronizing to Richard. It would have been easy for Mike to criticize Richard's handling of the studio manager. Instead, he asked probing questions and offered his ideas as advice.

Richard genuinely appreciated the fact that Mike asked him what actions he'd already taken to deal with the situation. Asking questions gave Richard the feeling that his friend was truly interested in his dilemma and not simply eager to show off how smart he was. Like most people, Richard hates it when others sum up a situation very rapidly and announce exactly what *ought* to be done.

Richard also appreciated the way Mike let him talk at length, making no move to cut him off. The result was that Richard didn't feel defensive as he poured out his tale, and also considered whatever advice Mike offered as well worth listening to because Mike carefully considered all angles before issuing an opinion. In general, the way Mike handled his friend Richard was obviously of value because it produced positive results.

Remember, criticism is a communication tool used for the purpose of bringing about a change to enable a person to better achieve a desired end result. If the criticism you're repeatedly offering someone is not bringing about positive changes, it's in your best interest—as well as the other party's—to try another approach.

Rather than examine another workplace scenario, let's assess a domestic situation that may seem all too familiar. Leslie and

Jonathan have been happily married for eight years. Both have successful careers and take their work quite seriously.

In the evening when they first get home, they typically enjoy exchanging mini-synopses of the events of their day.

Let's join them as they initiate a typical after-work conversation. Leslie begins by notifying her husband that she had an extremely tough day. "It began around mid-morning when we were given a four o'clock deadline on a huge report for one of our most demanding clients. I assigned Anna and Ken to the project because they're really the most experienced managers I have. But Anna really surprised me. After lunch, she walks into my office and brings up a *ridiculous* question. It was something that a real beginner in the department might ask. So I never told her the answer. Instead, I blurted out, 'Anna, all you need to do is think.' "

At this point, Jonathan interrupted Leslie and exclaimed, "I can't believe that's what you told her! You really weren't being fair. She was obviously under pressure and she certainly wouldn't have brought the question to you if she could have remembered the right answer."

Somewhat surprised by her husband's response, Leslie interjected, "Hold on, now; that wasn't even the point of the conversation. What I was saying was—" But Jonathan breaks in, "Well, it may not have been important to you at the time, but I don't know if you realize what a put-down that was for Anna."

Leslie, now enraged, says with a steely tone in her voice, "Just what are you accusing me of?" Jonathan proceeds, "Not letting people be—," but he stops himself in mid-sentence, because it's become evident to him that his wife is getting upset with his critical comments. Instead, he switches his focus from Anna to Leslie and mutters, "Wow, are you ever touchy tonight!" With a disgusted look on her face, Leslie responds, "Leave me alone, Jonathan—I've had enough garbage to contend with all day. I don't need to put up with anything more from you."

The two remain silent.

Prickly situations between loved ones can quickly become emotional, as you've just witnessed. What suggestions might you offer Leslie and Jonathan that would minimize the chances that another similar interaction will occur in the future?

Let's explore a few ideas. First, it's important for Jonathan and Leslie to view each other realistically. Marital partners are not able to always show that pleasant, polite posture that we try to maintain for friends and business associates. As a result, partners frequently are irritable, short-tempered, and insensitive. As the Simmons Market Research Bureau/Bright Enterprises criticism study revealed, marital couples typically criticize one another when they are tired and/or are in a bad mood. Chances are great that this is what occurred with Jonathan and Leslie. Under these circumstances, they need to be reminded that it's best not to place a value on the kind of exchange that just transpired between them.

It's also valuable for them to be aware that their conversation deteriorated because expectations were not clear. This probably sounds all too familiar. Leslie is looking for Jonathan to merely listen and not judge her comments. Jonathan, on the other hand, is seeking to show his support and he mistakenly does it by working with Leslie to resolve her office conflict. When expectations remain unclear, disappointments often result.

Most important, Leslie and Jonathan must try to listen without being judgmental. They need to focus on listening for the purpose of understanding. When the listener practices this, it's easier to be more compassionate. The nature and tone of the conversation change as each partner communicates in a more relaxed and comfortable manner.

As Jonathan and Leslie take another stab at improving their communication, it's important for them not to let any single disappointment discourage them because they are always blessed with the opportunity to try again.

Let us consider a situation involving a volunteer with a nagging problem to resolve.

Put yourself in the paid executive director's position as you try to work with Mr. Baumgarten, a volunteer who has logged many hours for the Heart Association. At frequent predepartmental and community outreach meetings, he always offers innovative ideas, so much so, that he dominates all conversations. Other volunteers are tired of having Mr. Baumgarten operate from a position of having all the answers, and have often complained to you in private about his monopolizing technique.

In an effort to handle this situation, you recognize that an even bigger question needs to be addressed first: "Do you criticize volunteers at all?" Those interviewed for this study had decidedly mixed responses. You should be aware that a number of those surveyed were either executive directors of volunteer agencies or high-level managers who had had experience working with volunteers and/or interns.

Virtually everyone queried agreed that the topic of criticizing volunteers was a sensitive one and that each situation would have to be handled individually, with careful consideration.

The problem is often one of ego. An executive in our survey whose opinion represented the majority felt that it's best *not* to criticize a volunteer by saying, "When people give their time freely, they often operate with a premise that says on some level, 'Since I'm volunteering my good services, I certainly don't need others to find fault with what I do!'"

Another manager of an organization that employs hundreds of volunteers in the course of a year offered this perspective to help determine whether or not criticism of volunteers has validity: "Ask yourself this one question: If volunteers do a lousy job on a particular project, will they still get a plaque or a certificate? Chances are great that you'll always get a 'yes' answer! So what's the point of criticizing? If you need to, said one association executive, then the best way to criticize is so they don't know it!"

However, one group of executives *did* believe that there is merit in judicious criticism of volunteers. One participant in our survey suggested, "You know, volunteers are *people*. If you can show them in an adult manner just what they could do better, they're generally quite receptive."

Steve Woolley, regional executive director for the U.S. Chamber of Commerce, agrees with this premise. He believes that *how* one criticizes a volunteer who is also a respected member of the community is the essential factor. "Because the people we deal with are prominent and highly visible, they are used to receiving criticism. When you do criticize a volunteer, you must begin only after giving the matter a great deal of thought. Your delivery must be professional and the giver must stay focused at all times on exactly what behavior is being criticized, and why the criticism is being given."

Criticism also needs to be stated in terms of its impact on goals and objectives. Woolley has no qualms about criticizing community leaders because, as an executive, he says, "my role is to protect the integrity of my organization. Because the volunteers respect the organization's image as well, they're likely to protect its leaders." Therefore, any criticism that a volunteer may receive is not a reflection of personal interest but, rather, an indication of interest in upholding and benefiting organizational integrity

In the case of Mr. Baumgarten, several factors need to be weighed: How significant *are* his contributions to the organization? How fragile do you suspect his ego might be? And can you tactfully suggest to him that there "may be others whose opinions are worth hearing, too"? It's possible that just such a simple statement prior to the next meeting could radically alter Mr. Baumgarten's style and make for a far more contented volunteer corps.

The examples presented here are by no means all-inclusive. The assorted issues and players involved were many, and the suggestions that have been offered are far from exhausted. There are no absolute rights or wrongs for handling these incidents; only less- or more-effective means of approaching them. As you studied each particular situation, it is to be hoped that you incorporated a number of quick charge techniques to help you maintain control.

When we are unable to handle situations as effectively as we'd like to, it's easy to turn that frustration into anger at ourselves. The Simmons/Bright research study indicated that frequent self-criticism is a common practice. Americans tend to be very hard on themselves, we discovered. But look back at the examples that Richard and Mike, Daniel and Ray, and even Alicia and Leo represent. From them we learned to change negative patterns once it becomes apparent that to do otherwise effects no improvement in the behavior of others.

Making mistakes in the work world is not only to be expected; it is to be appreciated, for mistakes serve as indicators of lessons to be learned. The next time you're put in the position of having to criticize a colleague, remember back to how you would have handled any one of the above examples—and proceed professionally, with caution. It's never too late to learn something new about improving your managerial skills.

THE SIMMONS MARKET RESEARCH BUREAU/ BRIGHT ENTERPRISES STUDY

The objective of our research was to investigate American managers' and professionals' problems and attitudes regarding criticism. We designed a questionnaire in conjunction with Simmons Market Research Bureau to address these specific subjects:

> criticism styles used with people who play different roles in our lives
> reactions to relationship-dependent criticism
> reactions to subject and situation-related criticism

A four-page questionnaire was mailed to a carefully selected sample of professionals or managers, selected from a database of 11,000 adults across the nation. Our overall response rate of 43% indicates a great interest in this subject on the part of our sample. A summary of our findings follows.

A. Reactions to Criticism

For both men and women, the most strongly resented criticism is that received from in-laws (24%), one's mate (22%) and subordinates (21%).

Men are more resentful of criticism from their children (24% vs. 14%) while women are more resentful of criticism from their parents (mother, 19% vs. 11%; father 14% vs. 6%).

While in-laws are most resented, they are least influential when criticizing. Only 14% of those surveyed think it is important to take corrective action when receiving criticism from an in-law, and only 11% frequently change their behavior as a result of criticism from an in-law.

One's boss, on the other hand, is most likely to elicit a change in one's behavior (61%).

Women are more apt to take corrective action when receiving criticism from co-workers (42% vs. 31%) and siblings (24% vs. 11%) and more likely than men to exhibit a change in behavior when being criticized by their mother (32% vs. 23%) and siblings (24% vs. 9%).

One's supervisory responsibilities in a job appear to be related to one's willingness to change his/her behavior as a result of criticism from someone in the work environment. Those who supervise others, as opposed to those who do not, are more likely to change their behavior when criticized by bosses (66% vs. 55%), co-workers (32% vs. 16%) and subordinates (30% vs. 6%).

Respondents react with the greatest hurt when they are criticized for something that questions their integrity (85%). Women react more sensitively than men for all the situations listed. Not suprisingly, supervisors are more upset by criticism about their job performance (80% vs. 67%) and management style (39% vs. 19%) than nonsupervisory personnel.

When asked how they react to criticism from different people, respondents were most likely to take it personally and react defensively if the person criticizing was a parent or in-law. Criticism from relations in the work environment and one's mate was most likely to result in questions that attempt to make the criticism clearer and more specific.

B. GIVING CRITICISM

More than one-fifth (24%) of professionals and managers find it just as difficult to give criticism as to receive it (22%). Women, however, find giving criticism much more difficult than do men (30% vs. 19%).

With regard to self-criticism, while more than three-quarters (77%) of respondents are hard on themselves, women tend to be more self-critical than men (85% vs. 71%).

Over half of those surveyed (51%) find it most difficult to criticize their boss. Women, compared with men, find it more difficult to give criticism to people of all types. Not surprisingly, so do people without supervisory responsibilities.

Most respondents indicate a difficult time when starting to criticize others regardless of whom the criticism is directed at. However, when they do begin to criticize, they try to start positively.

Children and mates tend to get the brunt of the criticism when respondents are tired or in a bad mood, or after tension builds.

TABLE 1

DEGREE OF RESENTMENT OF CRITICISM

From which of the people below do you most resent receiving criticism?

	Total %	Male %	Female %
In-laws	24	24	24
Mate	22	20	24
Subordinates	21	21	22
Children	19	24	14
Mother	14	11	19
Siblings	14	13	15
Co-workers	11	11	10
Boss	9	8	11
Father	9	6	14
Friends	8	9	6
Teachers	3	4	2

TABLE 2

DEGREE OF IMPORTANCE IN TAKING CORRECTIVE ACTION
WHEN RECEIVING CRITICISM

For which of the people listed below do you consider it most important to take corrective action when criticized?

	Total %	Male %	Female %
Boss	72	69	76
Mate	62	64	58
Friends	38	37	40
Co-workers	36	31	42
Children	33	33	34
Mother	33	34	32
Father	27	25	30
Teachers	26	25	28
Subordinates	24	27	22
Siblings	17	11	24
In-laws	14	13	16

TABLE 3

FREQUENCY OF CHANGE IN BEHAVIOR

For which of the people listed below do you actually change your behavior when criticized?

	Total %	Male %	Female %	Supervise Others Yes %	No %
Boss	61	58	63	66	55
Mate	54	55	53	56	52
Friends	33	27	40	34	31
Children	27	24	30	28	26
Mother	27	23	32	23	30
Co-workers	24	20	30	32	16
Teachers	24	24	25	26	23
Father	21	19	23	20	21
Subordinates	18	19	18	30	6
Siblings	16	9	24	16	15
In-laws	11	8	14	14	7

TABLE **4**

TYPE OF CRITICISM THAT WOULD HURT THE MOST

*If you were to be criticized for the following things, which would
hurt you the most?*

	Total %	Male %	Female %	Supervise Others Yes %	No %
Criticism that questions my integrity	85	81	90	88	81
Being criticized for my job performance	74	72	76	80	67
Being criticized for something that I know is untrue about myself	58	50	67	55	60
Being criticized for my knowledge and creativity	50	46	56	52	48
Being criticized for having a poor attitude	49	48	51	49	49
Being criticized for my appearance	42	33	54	44	41
Being criticized for something that was not my responsibility	39	36	43	39	38
Being criticized for the way I manage people	29	21	40	39	19
Being criticized because of my gender	23	16	33	22	24
Being criticized for something that I know is true about myself	14	10	20	16	13
Being criticized for something I was doing but was unaware of	14	9	20	14	14

TABLE 5

REACTION TO CRITICISM FROM DIFFERENT PEOPLE

How do you typically react when each person criticizes you?

	Mother %	Father %	Children %	Mate %	Friends %	Co-workers %	Boss %	Subordinates %	In-laws %	Teachers %	Siblings %
I take it personally	42	44	29	51	40	33	44	30	40	29	36
I become defensive	36	38	20	42	20	30	31	25	30	14	25
I ask questions to make the criticism clearer and more specific	32	36	43	58	56	59	66	53	26	46	43
I ask questions to sort out the intent behind the criticism	31	31	41	49	49	46	54	52	36	38	36
I tend not to listen	26	19	22	15	6	5	4	17	33	6	25
I quickly become upset	23	20	19	29	12	9	17	10	20	14	11
I become argumentative	21	24	24	34	6	15	10	14	15	9	24
I take steps to make sure that I am not personally rejected	18	22	24	29	30	23	22	19	9	9	16
I focus on quickly trying to find out how I can rectify the situation without wasting time to explore the entire situation	12	12	15	23	20	22	31	22	7	16	9
I accept the criticism without question	11	12	3	6	6	3	15	1	8	19	3
I start yelling	10	8	11	17	3	2	1	3	3	6	7
I don't admit the mistake and tend to blame others	8	4	5	10	7	8	2	2	5	1	8
I start crying	8	6	4	13	—	—	4	—	1	—	3

TABLE 6

DEGREE OF DIFFICULTY IN GIVING AND RECEIVING CRITICISM

How difficult is it for you to give criticism *and to* receive criticism?

	Total %	Male %	Female %
Very difficult—giving criticism	24	19	30
Very difficult—receiving criticism	22	20	24

TABLE 7

SELF-CRITICISM

According to the Random House College Dictionary, self-criticism *is defined as the tendency to find fault with one's actions and motives. How self-critical are you?*

	Total %	Male %	Female %
Too easy on self	2	4	—
Somewhat easy on self	21	25	15
Hard on self	48	42	57
Extremely hard on self	29	29	28

TABLE 8

DEGREE OF DIFFICULTY EXPERIENCED WHEN CRITICIZING DIFFERENT PEOPLE

Who is most difficult for you to criticize?

	Total %	Male %	Female %	Supervise Others Yes %	Supervise Others No %
Your boss	51	39	66	50	51
Someone older than you	37	29	47	34	40
Someone of a race different from yours	23	19	28	19	27
Your peers	22	17	28	17	27
Someone of the opposite sex	14	13	16	14	15
Someone of a religion different from yours	14	9	20	10	19
Someone of the same sex	12	5	22	11	14
Your subordinates	12	8	16	12	12
Someone younger than you	7	5	9	4	9

TABLE 9

CRITICISM STYLES USED WITH DIFFERENT PEOPLE

How do you tend to give criticism to each of the following people?

	Mother %	Father %	Children %	Mate %	Friends %	Co-workers %	Boss %	Subordinates %	In-laws %	Teachers %	Siblings %
I have a difficult time starting to criticize	34	41	15	30	38	32	39	31	34	42	27
I criticize with a positive start	31	31	42	38	47	47	37	54	25	32	31
I hesitate to criticize because I am unsure how the other person will respond	28	31	12	22	35	33	47	22	37	33	26
I criticize after waiting a prolonged period of time	26	28	20	36	33	28	24	26	21	16	20
I criticize by getting right to the point	25	26	34	36	20	24	23	36	12	19	18
I criticize indirectly	23	24	18	24	27	31	21	25	20	9	30
I criticize after tension builds	14	16	24	49	15	23	24	18	17	4	25
I criticize impulsively	13	8	41	26	7	8	6	7	7	4	26
I criticize by joking	13	18	24	33	36	27	17	20	14	9	31
I criticize when tired or in a bad mood	13	11	45	53	15	9	8	12	6	4	13
I criticize by yelling	5	8	26	16	1	1	1	3	—	—	6
I criticize and forget to give examples	4	4	14	13	5	3	4	6	—	2	6
I criticize only after being told to	2	2	5	4	3	6	5	7	5	5	4

ABOUT THE AUTHOR

DEBORAH BRIGHT is the president of Bright Enterprises, Inc., a New York–based resource company specializing in improving performance and enhancing the quality of management in business and industry. Some of her clients include the FBI, where she helps train law enforcement officers from around the world. She trains all new national account managers for AT&T. IBM brought her in for several management training sessions, and she has just completed negotiations on a contract with the Professional Golfers' Association of America (PGA), training professional golfers in the areas of enhancing personal effectiveness and managing business effectively.

An unpublicized aspect of Deborah Bright's work is training amateur and professional athletes, among them the Detroit Tigers, in maximizing their performance in highly competitive situations. She was once ranked among the top ten U.S. women divers, and her impressive career in platform and springboard diving led to competition in the Olympic Trials.

In addition to conducting training programs as a part of the Bright Learning Center, Deborah Bright is the author of the best-seller, *Creative Relaxation: Turning Your Stress into Positive Energy* and *Gearing Up for the Fast Lane: New Tools for Management in a High-Tech World.*

Deborah earned her doctorate in adult education from Arizona State University and is currently an adjunct professor on the faculty at New York University, where she teaches courses on "Turning Job Stress into Positive Energy" and "Managing for Exceptional Performance."

Additional copies of *Criticism in Your Life* may be ordered by sending a check for $9.95 (please add the following for postage and handling: $1.50 for the first copy, $.50 for each added copy) to:

MasterMedia Limited
16 East 72nd Street
New York, NY 10021
(212) 260-5600

Deborah Bright is available for speeches and workshops. Please contact MasterMedia's Speakers' Bureau for availability and fee arrangements. Call Tony Colao at (201) 359-1612.

Other MasterMedia Books:

THE PREGNANCY AND MOTHERHOOD DIARY: Planning the First Year of Your Second Career, by Susan Schiffer Stautberg, is the first and only undated appointment diary that shows how to manage pregnancy and career. ($12.95 spiralbound)

CITIES OF OPPORTUNITY: Finding the Best Place to Work, Live and Prosper in the 1990's and Beyond, by Dr. John Tepper Marlin, explores the job and living options for the next decade and into the next century. This consumer guide and handbook, written by one of the world's experts on cities, selects and features 46 American cities and metropolitan areas. ($13.95 paper, $24.95 cloth)

THE DOLLARS AND SENSE OF DIVORCE, by Dr. Judith Briles, is the first book to combine practical tips on overcoming the legal hurdles and planning finances before, during, and after divorce. ($10.95 paper)

OUT THE ORGANIZATION: How Fast Could You Find a New Job?, by Madeleine and Robert Swain, is written for the millions of Americans whose jobs are no longer safe, whose companies are not loyal, and who face futures of uncertainty. It gives advice on finding a new job or starting your own business. ($11.95 paper, $17.95 cloth)

AGING PARENTS AND YOU: A Complete Handbook to Help You Help Your Elders Maintain a Healthy, Productive and Independent Life, by Eugenia Anderson-Ellis and Marsha Dryan, is a complete guide to providing care to aging relatives. It gives practical advice and resources to the adults who are helping their elders lead productive and independent lives. ($9.95 paper)

BEYOND SUCCESS: How Volunteer Service Can Help You Begin Making a Life Instead of Just a Living, by John F. Raynolds III and Eleanor Raynolds, C.B.E., is a unique how-to book targeted to business and professional people considering volunteer work, senior citizens who wish to fill leisure time meaningfully, and students trying out various career options. The book is filled with interviews with celebrities, CEOs, and average citizens who talk about the benefits of service work. ($9.95 paper, $19.95 cloth)

MANAGING IT ALL: Time-Saving Ideas for Career, Family, Relationships and Self, by Beverly Benz Treuille and Susan Schiffer Stautberg, is written for women who are juggling careers and families. Over 200 career women (ranging from a TV anchorwoman to an investment banker) were interviewed. The book contains many humorous anecdotes on saving time and improving the quality of life for self and family. ($9.95 paper)

REAL LIFE 101: (Almost) Surviving Your First Year Out of College, by Susan Kleinman, supplies welcome advice to those facing "real life" for the first time, focusing on work, money, health, and how to deal with freedom and responsibility. ($9.95 paper)

YOUR HEALTHY BODY, YOUR HEALTHY LIFE: How to Take Control of Your Medical Destiny, by Donald B. Louria, M.D., provides precise advice that will help you to keep illness at bay. Dr. Louria, the author of four books and hundreds of articles for professional journals, focuses on nutrition, self-diagnosis, and exercise to combat the common sources of sickness and death. ($12.95 paper)

THE CONFIDENCE FACTOR: How Self-Esteem Can Change Your Life, by Judith Briles, is based on a nationwide survey of 6,000 men and women. Briles explores why women so often feel a lack of self-confidence and have a poor opinion of themselves. She offers step-by-step advice on becoming the person you want to be. ($18.95 cloth)